Let's Learn Together NEW TESTAMENT

Conversation Starters and Activities to Enrich Your Family's Study of Come, Follow Me

Rebecca Irvine

Chetnole House Publishing, LLC

Published by Chetnole House Publishing, LLC

Mesa, Arizona

Paperback edition

Interior design by Rebecca Irvine

Cover design by Rebecca Irvine

ISBN 978-1-7323747-2-0

For Devyn.

Table of Contents

1. Jesus Christ
2. Zacharias
3. Elisabeth
4. Angel Gabriel
5. Mary, Mother of Jesus Christ
6. Joseph
7. Birth of Jesus
8. Passover
9. Jesus in the Temple at 12
10. Nazareth
11. John the Beloved
12. Mark
13. John the Baptist
14. John the Baptist Preaches
15. Baptism of Jesus
16. Jordan River
17. Pharisees
18. Sadducees
19. Jerusalem
20. Jesus is Tempted
21. Water Turned to Wine
22. Capernaum
23. Nicodemus
24. Samaritan Woman at the Well
25. Sermon on the Mount
26. Blind Man in Bethsaida
27. Pool of Siloam
28. Centurion's Servant Healed

29. Daughter of Jairus
30. Healing at Pool of Bethesda
31. Bleeding Woman Healed
32. Widow of Nain
33. Calling of the Apostles
34. Matthew (Levi)
35. James the Great
36. Parable of the Sower
37. Parable of the Wheat and Tares
38. Parable of the Mustard Seed
39. Parable of the Hidden Treasure
40. Mary Magdalene
41. Simon Peter
42. Simon Peter's Catch
43. Five Loaves and Two Fishes
44. Jesus Walks on Water
45. Sea of Galilee
46. Jesus Calms the Storm
47. Mount of Transfiguration
48. Mount Tabor
49. Caesarea Philippi
50. Samaria
51. Parable of the Good Samaritan
52. Jericho
53. Mary and Martha
54. Healing of Blind Man Since Birth
55. Parable of the Lost Sheep
56. Parable of the Foolish Rich Man
57. Parable of the Prodigal Son
58. Parable of the Lost Coin
59. Ten Lepers Healed

60. Martha
61. Mary (Sister of Martha)
62. Lazarus
63. Cursing the Fig Tree
64. Triumphal Entry
65. Herod's Temple
66. Jesus Cleanses the Temple
67. Parable of the Two Sons
68. Parable of the Ten Virgins
69. Parable of the Sheep and Goats
70. Olivet Discourse
71. Parable of the Budding Fig Tree
72. Parable of the Talents
73. Last Supper
74. Intercessory Prayer
75. Judas Iscariot
76. Mount of Olives
77. Gethsemane
78. Sanhedrin
79. Annas
80. Joseph ben Caiaphas
81. Trials of Christ
82. Procla (Pontius Pilate's Wife)
83. Pontius Pilate
84. Simon of Cyrene
85. Jesus is Crucified
86. Calvary
87. Joseph of Arimathea
88. Jesus is Resurrected
89. Joanna
90. Thomas

91. Luke
92. Ascension
93. Pentecost
94. Matthias
95. Paul (Saul)
96. Saul's Conversion
97. Ananias
98. Stephen
99. Philip
100. Tabitha
101. Council at Jerusalem
102. Rhoda
103. Silas
104. Barnabas
105. Antioch
106. Paul and Silas in Jail
107. Mars Hill
108. Paul is Shipwrecked
109. Apollos
110. Priscilla and Aquila
111. Claudius Caesar
112. Rome
113. Epistles
114. Epistle to the Romans
115. First Epistle to the Corinthians
116. Second Epistle to the Corinthians
117. Emperor Nero
118. Epistle to the Galatians
119. Epistle to the Ephesians
120. Armor of God
121. Epistle to the Philippians

122. Epistle to the Colossians
123. Epistles to the Thessalonians
124. Timothy
125. Epistles to Timothy
126. Titus
127. Epistle to Titus
128. Philemon
129. Epistle to Philemon
130. Epistle to the Hebrews
131. James the Just
132. Epistle of James
133. Epistles of Peter
134. Epistles of John
135. Jude (Brother of James)
136. Epistle of Jude
137. John the Beloved
138. Aegean Isle of Patmos
139. Book of Revelation
140. Apocalypse
141. Herod the Great
142. Bethlehem
143. Shepherds
144. Wise Men
145. Simeon
146. Anna the Prophetess
147. War in Heaven
148. Babylon
149. Angel in the Midst of Heaven
150. Book of Life

5 Bonus Topics:

151. Egypt
152. Tiberius Caesar
153. Andrew
154. Miracle of the Swine
155. Parable of the House Built Upon a Rock

1. Jesus Christ

Jesus Christ is the Son of God and the central figure of the New Testament; His life and teachings are detailed in the four gospels. Christ's doctrine and example demonstrate how to find lasting happiness in life. At the epitome of His ministry, Jesus willingly took upon Himself the sins of the world in Gethsemane, then completed His sacrifice on the cross at Calvary. And, in fulfillment of prophecy, He overcame death through joyful resurrection. Christ's Atonement makes possible God's plan for the redemption of His children.

Discussion Questions:

1. Consider some of the names used for Jesus Christ in the New Testament, such as Lamb of God, Begotten Son, Bread of Life, and Holy One of Israel. Which names do you appreciate the most? What do these different names teach or help you to understand about Christ?

2. How has the life of Jesus Christ influenced you personally? What advice would you give to someone who wanted to build a more personal relationship with the Savior?

3. Which New Testament story of the Savior is your favorite? Why?

For Children:

Learn the song "Tell Me the Stories of Jesus" (*CS* p. 57). Let the children tell which story about Jesus they like the best (use pictures from the Gospel Art Kit on the Church website to help provide options if the children are younger). Ask, why is that story your favorite? How do you feel about Jesus Christ?

2. Zacharias

Zacharias was the father of John the Baptist. As a priest, Zacharias was chosen to serve in the temple. During his service he saw the angel Gabriel standing to the right of the golden altar. Gabriel told Zacharias that his wife, Elisabeth, would have a son, whom they were to name John; this son would be the forerunner of the Savior. Because of his and Elizabeth's age, Zacharias asked how he would know if the prophecy was true. In response the angel struck him dumb as a sign. Zacharias was unable to speak until after the birth of John.

Discussion Questions:

1. What do you learn from the difference between Mary's and Zacharias's responses to Gabriel's annunciations? Why do some readily accept God's revelation while others question?

2. Why do you think Gabriel took away Zacharias's ability to speak as a sign of the truth of the prophecy? What other signs might have been used instead?

3. At the time of Gabriel's appearance to Zacharias in the temple "the whole multitude of the people were praying without" (Luke 1:10). What experiences have you had praying with others? How did the Lord respond to your prayers?

For Children:

Choose a favorite card or board game that the children like to play, but add a new rule: no one is allowed to talk with their mouth while playing the game. Encourage the children to use gestures or write notes to communicate as they play. After, tell the story of Zacharias seeing Gabriel in the temple and being struck dumb temporarily. Ask, why do you think Gabriel took away Zacharias's ability to speak as a sign of the truth of the prophecy? What other signs might have been used instead?

3. Elisabeth

Elisabeth was the mother of John the Baptist. She was also a cousin of Mary, the mother of Jesus Christ. In Elisabeth's old age she had given up the hope of ever having children. However, while her husband Zacharias was serving in the temple, the angel Gabriel appeared and prophesied she would bear a son who would be the forerunner to the Savior. Shortly afterward Elisabeth conceived. During her pregnancy Mary came to visit and Elisabeth bore testimony that her cousin's unborn child would be the Christ child.

Discussion Questions:

1. What do you think Elisabeth's response might have been when she first learned about Gabriel's prophecy? How might she have responded on first learning she was pregnant?

2. Elisabeth had given up on the righteous desire to have children. What lessons can we learn about faith, promises, and prayer from Elisabeth's story?

3. When Mary comes to visit, Elisabeth is "filled with the Holy Ghost" (Luke 1:41). Why do you think the mere presence of Mary brought the spirit so strongly?

For Children:

Explain to the children that cousins are relatives whose parents are siblings (brothers and/or sisters). Look at family pictures of cousins (or your own or the children's). Share memories and stories of time spent with cousins. Remind the children that Mary and Elisabeth in the New Testament were cousins, despite a wide age gap. These women spent three months together before they became the mothers of John the Baptist and Jesus Christ. Ask, what do you think this time was like for these cousins? How do you think they spent their time? What memories might they have made?

4. Angel Gabriel

The angel Gabriel appears in both the Old and New Testaments. In the Old Testament he is sent to Daniel; in the New Testament he announces the impending births of both John the Baptist and Jesus Christ. In visiting Zacharias in the temple, Gabriel gave him a sign of the truth of his words and struck Zacharias dumb. In latter-days, Joseph Smith revealed the angel Gabriel to be Noah, who stands second only to Adam in holding the priesthood keys of salvation (HC 3:386).

Discussion Questions:

1. Why do you think God sent Noah/Gabriel to announce the impending births of John and Jesus? Why did he receive this honor?

2. Gabriel tells Zacharias, "For with God nothing shall be impossible" (Luke 1:37). What does this declaration mean to you? What is something impossible you would like to see happen?

3. Gabriel tells both Zacharias and Mary to "fear not" (Luke 1:13) when they first see him. Describe how would you feel if you saw an angel? How would you react?

For Children:

Use sidewalk chalk and draw angel wings on the ground. Take pictures of family members laying on top of the wings. Ask the children what angels they have heard of; help them brainstorm angels they may have heard of from the scriptures or elsewhere. Tell the story of the angel Gabriel appearing to either Zacharias or Mary. Ask, how would you feel if you saw an angel? How would you react?

5. Mary, Mother of Jesus Christ

Mary, of King David's lineage, was the virgin mother of Jesus Christ. Her matriarchal role was prophesied by Isaiah, King Benjamin, Alma, and others. As the betrothed wife of Joseph, Mary was visited by Gabriel, who announced her miraculous calling. Although her pregnancy caused Joseph hesitancy, they married and traveled to Bethlehem where Jesus was born. Although few details exist, Mary appears to have played a key role in the life of the Savior. While on the cross, Jesus took time to ensure Mary would be cared for by the Apostle John.

Discussion Questions:

1. In Nephi's vision Mary is described as "beautiful and fair" (1 Ne. 11:13–20). Do you think this description is idealized? Why or why not? What do you think she may have looked like?

2. When Mary agreed to Gabriel's annunciation and God's plan for her life, what kinds of personal priorities, if any, did Mary have to abandon? How challenging might this have been for her?

3. Why do you think the prophets prophesied about Jesus's mother? What influence might Mary have had on the growth and development of Jesus?

For Children:

Sing or read some nursery rhymes, including "Mary had a Little Lamb" and "Mary, Mary Quite Contrary." Explain that historically Mary has a commonly used name, partially because it is the name of the Savior's mother. Read Alma 7:10 where it is prophesied the Savior's mother will be named Mary. Ask, why do you think the prophets prophesied about Jesus's mother? What influence do you think Mary had on Jesus?

6. Joseph

Joseph, as an heir of royal descent through the Davidic line, is the stepfather of Jesus Christ. He worked as a carpenter for a living. Betrothed to Mary, Joseph was surprised to learn of her pregnancy and considered putting her "away privily" (Matt. 1:19) until an angel appeared to him and explained that Mary's child would be the Savior. Joseph followed the spiritual prompting to take his family into Egypt, saving Jesus's life. It is likely Joseph died before Jesus's ministry began; it is implied that he was dead before the Crucifixion.

Discussion Questions:

1. The angel convinced Joseph, through his dream, to take Mary as his wife. Do you think Joseph could have been convinced of God's plan in any other way? Why or why not?

2. In what ways was Joseph's life blessed by humbly following the guidance of the Lord? How can we learn to be humble like Joseph?

3. What difficulties or challenges might Joseph have experienced as a stepparent? What can we learn from Joseph's care for Mary and Jesus?

For Children:

Have the children pretend to be carpenters using toy or age-appropriate tools. Explain that Jesus's stepfather, Joseph, was a carpenter by trade. Review the story of Joseph following a prompting from the Holy Ghost to take Mary and Jesus to Egypt. Ask, why did Joseph take Mary and Jesus to Egypt? How did Joseph help protect baby Jesus and Mary?

7. Birth of Jesus

Jesus Christ was born in Bethlehem, a small city that had been the home of many of the Savior's ancestors, including Ruth, Boaz, Jesse, and King David. At the time of Jesus's birth, a census of Judea (taken for tax purposes) was underway, and Joseph had taken Mary to Bethlehem to register in their ancestral home. While there, Mary gave birth in a stable "because there was no room for them in the inn" (Luke 2:7). Shortly after the birth a new star was seen in the sky and shepherds came to find the Christ child.

Discussion Questions:

1. How do you think Mary and Joseph each felt about traveling and her pregnancy? How challenging might the journey have been for them?

2. Do you think someone might have made room if they had known more about the child Mary was carrying? Why or why not?

3. The Savior's birth story is unexpected considering His deity. What's your favorite "unexpected" detail in the Nativity story? What detail would you change if you had the chance to do so?

For Children:

Have the children color a picture of the Nativity while you read the story from Luke 2. Ask, what is your favorite part of the story of Jesus's birth? Would you rather have been a shepherd, an angel, or one of the animals in the manger? Why?

8. Passover

The Passover is a Jewish holiday celebrating the release of Israel from captivity in Egypt. Moses plead with Pharaoh to let the Jews go free and cursed the land with a series of plagues. Each time Pharaoh refused. A final tenth plague promised death of any firstborn male in the home. Moses told the Israelites to paint the blood of a blemish-free male lamb on the lintel and side posts of their doorway for protection. The Lord promised, "When I see the blood, I will pass over you, and the plague shall not be upon you to destroy you, when I smite the land of Egypt" (Ex. 12:13). In the New Testament, Jesus's family traveled to Jerusalem to celebrate the Passover, and the crucifixion of the Savior took place at this time.

Discussion Questions:

1. In His youth, Jesus's family made the journey to Jerusalem to celebrate Passover each year. How do you think this tradition influenced the Savior? How have the family traditions of your youth influenced you?

2. What do Passover and Easter have in common? How do they differ?

3. Jesus's Crucifixion took place during Passover. What symbolism do you see in this? What can we learn from it?

For Children:

Give each child a paper plate. Have them draw the common dishes served during a Passover meal, including roast lamb, bitter herbs, unleavened bread, wine (or grape juice). Tell them the story of the original Passover and explain that Jesus's family celebrated the holiday by traveling to Jerusalem each year. Ask, what do you think Jesus liked about going to Jerusalem each year to celebrate Passover? What family traditions or holidays do you look forward to each year? Why?

9. Jesus in the Temple at 12

The year Jesus turned 12 His family made their annual trip to Jerusalem for the Passover, but on the way home His parents discovered He was not in their company of travelers. Mary and Joseph turned back and searched the city. Finally, they found Him in the temple sitting and talking with the doctors, who were amazed at Jesus's understanding of the scriptures and doctrine. Mary and Joseph reprimanded Jesus for not staying with the family, but Jesus told them He needed to be about His "Father's business" (Luke 2:49).

Discussion Questions:

1. Why do you think Luke included this story in his Gospel? What is significant about Jesus talking with the doctors in the temple?

2. When Jesus's parents found Him, He was "sitting in the midst of the doctors, both hearing them, and asking them questions" (Luke 2:46). What do you think Jesus was trying to do? Was He teaching or learning? Why?

3. What do you think Jesus was like in his pre-teen and teenage years? At what age do you think He began to fully understand His role in the Plan of Salvation? Explain.

For Children:

Hide a picture of Jesus and let your children search for it. Let the children each take a turn hiding the picture while the others search. After, share the story of Jesus "lost" in Jerusalem at the temple when He was 12. Ask, why do you think Jesus went to the temple? Was He teaching or learning there? Why?

10. Nazareth

Nazareth, a town near Galilee, was the childhood home of Jesus Christ; both Mary and Joseph were living there at the time of the annunciation. The Savior became known as Jesus of Nazareth as He traveled during His ministry. In the synagogue in Nazareth Jesus taught that Isaiah's prophecy had been fulfilled in Him: "The Lord hath anointed me to preach good tidings unto the meek; he hath sent me to bind up the brokenhearted, to proclaim liberty to the captives" (Isaiah 61:1). The people of Nazareth rejected this teaching, after which there is no record of Christ's return.

Discussion Questions:

1. Why do you think the people of Nazareth rejected the Savior when He declared Himself as the fulfillment of Isaiah's prophecy? Do you think Jesus ever returned after being cast out of the city?

2. Despite Nazareth's rejection of Jesus, He became well-known for being from there. Why was the Lord's hometown so closely associated with His name?

3. Matthew 2:23 states, "And he came and dwelt in a city called Nazareth: that it might be fulfilled which was spoken by the prophets, He shall be called a Nazarene"; however, no such prophecy is found in scripture. What do you think happened to this prophecy? Which Old Testament prophet is most likely to have given such a prophecy?

For Children:

Show the children where Nazareth is found on a map of Israel. Help the children to learn the four directions of the compass by pointing out the following: Tyre is north of Nazareth, Jerusalem is south, Mount Tabor is east, and the Mediterranean Sea is west. Explain that during Jesus's ministry he traveled many different directions to teach people. Ask, why do you think they called Him Jesus of Nazareth? How do you think Jesus felt about Nazareth?

11. John the Beloved

John the Beloved is the brother of James; both brothers were sons of Zebedee and worked as fishermen prior to following Jesus. John is the author of five books in the New Testament, including St. John, the three Epistles of John, and the Book of Revelation. Peter, James, and John served together as leaders over the Church after Christ's resurrection. After Peter's death (in about A.D. 67) John would have been the senior and presiding apostle. For a time, John was exiled on the isle of Patmos, where he received the Book of Revelation.

Discussion Questions:

1. John refers to himself as "the disciple whom Jesus loved" (John 13:23). What does this self-description reveal to you about John's personality? What might it say about his relationship with Christ?

2. John is the only one of the Twelve recorded as being present during the Crucifixion. Why do you think he stayed?

3. James and John both came from a successful family of fishermen. What do you think it was like for them to leave their profession behind to follow Jesus? What would be most challenging about doing this?

For Children:

Make a fishing pole from a dowel and string; attach a magnet to the end of the string. Cut out a variety of paper fish and place a paper clip on each one. Let the children go fishing with the pole and the fish. After, explain that some of Jesus's disciples, including John, were fishermen before they followed Him. Ask, what do you think it was like for them to leave their profession behind to follow Jesus? Was it easy or hard for them? Why?

12. Mark

Although the ancient manuscripts of the Gospel of Mark include a heading with this attribution, scholars assume the author was John Mark, whose mother welcomed Christians into her Jerusalem home (Acts 12:12). John Mark was a cousin of Barnabas; together they accompanied Paul as missionaries. Papias (a contemporary Greek Bishop) indicated John Mark served as Peter's interpreter. Mark likely wrote his Gospel around 70 A.D. in Rome.

Discussion Questions:

1. The identity of Mark is somewhat uncertain. Why do you think the Lord has not made more known about this faithful writer? How important is recognition in the service of God?

2. John Mark served a mission with his cousin. What would it be like to get to go on a mission with a sibling or cousin? Which sibling or cousin would you most like to serve with?

3. Mark writes that one of the signs of those who follow Jesus is "they shall lay hands on the sick, and they shall recover" (Mark 16:18). Share a time when you received or witnessed a blessing of the sick. What happened?

For Children:

Teach the children how to say the word "scripture" in different languages [i.e., *sagrada escritura* (Spanish), *scrittura* (Italian), *seisho* (Japanese), or *skriften* (Swedish)]. Explain that knowing how to change a word to a different language is called translating, and people who do this are called translators. Tell the children that the writer of the Gospel of Mark in the New Testament was known to be a translator. Mark served as a missionary and shared the gospel in different languages. Ask, what languages do you think would be interesting to learn? In what languages would you like to teach others the gospel?

13. John the Baptist

John the Baptist was a cousin and prophesied forerunner of the Savior. John's birth was announced by the angel Gabriel and his parents conceived miraculously in their old age. Raised in the wilderness, from his youngest years, John was filled with the Holy Ghost and learned to preach with great power. Many wondered if he himself was the promised Savior. At the start of Jesus's ministry, He requested baptism of John in the Jordan River. Later, John was put in prison and was beheaded.

Discussion Questions:

1. A forerunner is someone who comes ahead to prepare the way for another. Why do you think forerunners are important? Why does the Lord use forerunners?

2. John was raised in the desert wearing camel skin and eating honey and locust. Why do you think his parents raised him this way? What unique or different parenting styles have your parents or grandparents used?

3. What do you imagine John and Jesus's relationship was like growing up? How would you have felt if the Savior was your cousin?

For Children:

Look at the picture of John the Baptist teaching the gospel (inside the back cover of the February 2011 Friend magazine). Explain that by preparing the way for Jesus, John was a forerunner. Ask, how did John help prepare the way for Jesus? What can we do to share the gospel with others?

14. John the Baptist Preaches

John the Baptist's ministry portended Jesus, but was parallel to the Savior's, too. John came forth from the desert well prepared to preach repentance to the Jews. He ate foods associated with being clean and wore clothing traditionally associated with prophets. His preaching attracted large crowds as he taught near the river Jordan. Jesus said of him, "Among those that are born of women there is not a greater prophet" (Luke 7:28).

Discussion Questions:

1. John the Baptist was known for being strange in the food he ate, clothing he wore, and wilderness living. Brainstorm famous people in today's world are considered strange for these types of attributes. How do you think someone like John the Baptist would be perceived today?

2. John the Baptist testified Jesus was the "Lamb of God" (John 1:29). What did John mean by this? How is Jesus like a lamb?

3. John the Baptist called to repentance authority figures in Jerusalem, both those of the Jewish faith and those in government. How do you think these authority figures reacted to John? How would you feel if someone told you to repent?

For Children:

John the Baptist was famous for wearing a camel hair coat. Find a coloring page of John the Baptist and have the children glue small pieces of brown yarn on the coat to represent the camel hair. While waiting for the glue to dry, tell the children about John the Baptist's ministry and testimony of Jesus as the "Lamb of God" (Luke 7:28). Ask, what was John the Baptist's special mission? Why did he call people to repentance?

15. Baptism of Jesus

Jesus asked his cousin, John the Baptist, to baptize Him in the Jordan River. At first John refused, saying, "I have need to be baptized of thee, and comest thou to me?" Jesus told John that He needed to be baptized "fulfil all righteousness," after which John agreed to baptize Him. Immediately after the baptism, the Holy Ghost appeared in the form of a dove and a voice from heaven said, "This is my beloved Son, in whom I am well pleased" (Matt. 3:13-17).

Discussion Questions:

1. Why did Jesus go to John to be baptized? What was His reasoning? Why didn't John want to baptize Jesus? How long do you think it took Jesus to convince John to baptize Him?

2. Share a time when you attended someone's baptism. How was the service similar or different to the Savior's baptism? In what way(s) you feel the presence of the Holy Ghost?

3. How do the Holy Ghost and Heavenly Father affirm Jesus's true identity? What was their purpose in doing this? What promptings or feelings has the Holy Ghost given you personally in affirmation of Jesus's identity?

For Children:

Use the sing-along video of the Primary song "Baptism" (CS p. 100; included on the Church website in the Gospel Media section) to learn about the baptism of Jesus Christ. After, review the story from the scriptures. Ask, why was John the Baptist hesitant to baptize Jesus at first? Why did Jesus want to get baptized?

16. Jordan River

The Jordan River is a prominent geographical feature in both the Old and New Testaments. The Jordan runs about 150 miles north to south through the Sea of Galilee down to the Dead Sea. In the New Testament, John the Baptist uses the Jordan to baptize the Savior; afterward John bore record of Jesus as the Lamb of God. During His ministry Jesus frequently crossed the Jordan or took refuge along the shoreline. He healed a blind man by sending him to wash his eyes in the Jordan after anointing them with clay.

Discussion Questions:

1. The Jordan River is where John baptized people unto repentance. Share the location and occasion of your own baptism. What do you remember? How did you feel?

2. A number of Biblical stories take place at or near the Jordan River (e.g., Joshua parts the Jordan River, Naaman washes seven times in the Jordan, Jesus is baptized there, etc.). Which of these stories is your favorite? Why?

3. The Jordan River has the lowest elevation of any river in the world. How might this be symbolic of the Savior? Explain.

For Children:

Visit a riverbank or canal and enjoy the water, possibly participating in some water sports. While there, share the story of the baptism of Jesus by John the Baptist. Explain that this took place in the Jordan River. For older children ask, where were you baptized? What do you remember? For younger children ask, where will you be baptized? What happens at a baptism?

17. Pharisees

During the Old Testament, a group developed from the pious who objected to the religious policies of their leaders. This group of conservative separatists became known as Pharisees. "The Pharisees now took a leading role in Jewish life. Being very conservative, they felt that the ancient law must be reinterpreted to apply to new questions and problems. This belief gave rise to scores of regulations to observe every minute detail of the law" (Dahl, P. "The Setting of the New Testament," *Ensign*, Jul. 1983, 68). During the Savior's ministry Pharisaical beliefs prevented many of the people from recognizing Christ as the Messiah.

Discussion Questions:

1. Christ told the Pharisees their outer "cup" was clean, but the inner part was "full of ravening and wickedness" (Luke 11:39). What do you think Christ was trying to teach? How can we ensure our heart and behavior are better aligned?

2. In Luke 12 Jesus uses the metaphor of yeast to describe the sins of the Pharisees. What point is Jesus trying to make? What can we learn from this ourselves?

3. After Christ healed the blind man, the Pharisees were upset the healing took place on the Sabbath. Where were the Pharisees' priorities in this story? What kept the Pharisees from having a proper response to the miracle?

For Children:

After having a meal, have the children help hand wash some of the dirty dishes in the sink. Demonstrate the importance of cleaning both the inside and outside of each dish. Share the story of Jesus having a meal with some Pharisees who criticized the Savior for not washing before the meal. In response the Savior said, "Now do ye Pharisees make clean the outside of the cup and the platter; but your inward part is full of ravening and wickedness" (Luke 11:39). Ask, what do you think Christ was trying to teach? How can we have clean hearts?

18. Saddučees

The Sadducees were a small group of Jewish aristocracy members. As rivals of the Pharisees, the Sadducees claimed their birth and socioeconomic position gave them power. Their beliefs were rooted strongly and in Mosaic Law, which they interpreted literally. They did not believe in a resurrection of the dead. As high priests during the life of Christ, the Sadducees managed the temple in Jerusalem. Despite their strict religious beliefs, the Sadducees were well-known for compromising with the Romans; as a result, many considered them hypocrites.

Discussion Questions:

1. In Matthew 16 the Sadducees ask the Savior to show them a sign, to which Christ says, "There shall no sign be given unto it, but the sign of the prophet Jonas" (Matt. 16:4). What is the sign of Jonas? What do you think the Savior is trying to teach the Sadducees?

2. The Sadducees tried to trick Jesus into answering challenging doctrinal questions, to which the Savior responds, "Do ye not therefore err, because ye know not the scriptures?" (Mark 12:24). What can we learn from this response about finding answers to gospel questions?

3. The Pharisees and Sadducees were rivals. Why do you think they joined together against the Savior?

For Children:

Buy a pack of gum to use as an object lesson. Before showing it to the children, carefully remove the gum from the wrappers and replace it with cardboard or heavy weight paper. Reload it into the packaging. Offer the children a stick of gum and wait for their reactions. Explain that when someone pretends to be one way, but then behaves a different way (like the gum), this is called being a hypocrite. Tell about the Sadducees in the New Testament, who Jesus called hypocrites. Ask, what is wrong with being a hypocrite? How does the Savior want us to behave?

19. Jerusalem

About 1000 years before the birth of Christ, King David conquered the city of Jebus (Zion) and made it the capital of Israel, renaming it Jerusalem. After Solomon built a temple, the city became a mecca. The Savior was brought to the temple in Jerusalem as a child, and his family came regularly to attend festivals. Jerusalem was a key location during Jesus's ministry: He preached and healed there; He cleansed the temple; and His trial and crucifixion took place in Jerusalem. The Pentecost described in Acts 2 also took place here.

Discussion Questions:

1. Jerusalem was a place of danger for the Savior, but He frequently returned there. Why did Jesus keep returning to Jerusalem? What was He trying to accomplish by going there?

2. Jesus mourned over Jerusalem as He considered its past and future. What about Jerusalem caused Jesus to feel sad? Why did Jesus predict Jerusalem would be destroyed?

3. Which of the signs of the Second Coming that will take place in Jerusalem are you most interested in seeing occur (e.g., water come from under the temple mount, earthquake, Armageddon, New Jerusalem built, etc.)? Explain.

For Children:

Look at some artistic renditions of Herod's Temple, which was being rebuilt during the Savior's life on earth. After, look at some of the photographs of the temple today. Have the children look for similarities and differences. Explain that Jesus often visited Jerusalem growing up and He went there during His ministry to preach and heal people. It was in Jerusalem that Jesus was tried and sentenced to be crucified. Ask, if Jerusalem was a dangerous place for Jesus, why did he keep returning? How might Jerusalem have been special to Jesus?

20. Jesus is Tempted

Near the beginning of His ministry, the Savior went out into the wilderness to be near God and to fast 40 days and nights. At the end of this time, Satan tempted Jesus three times. First, when he was hungry, Satan tempted Jesus to turn stones into bread. Next, Satan took Jesus up onto the pinnacle of the temple and tempted Him to cast Himself off so the angels would save Him. Lastly, Satan tempted Jesus to worship him in return for worldly glory. Each time Jesus refused, and He ultimately cast Satan out.

Discussion Questions:

1. The first temptation Christ experiences is physical in nature. What physical temptations do people frequently experience? How can we learn to master our physical appetites?

2. The second temptation Christ has appeals to pride. What temptations do people experience because of their pride? How can we learn to better recognize and avoid temptations of this sort?

3. The third temptation Satan uses is that of materialism. What materialistic temptations do you see Satan using today? How can we avoid being caught in materialistic lures?

For Children:

Read Matthew 4:1-11 together with the children to teach them the story of Jesus being tempted by Satan (note: the JST adds helpful clarification to verse 1). After, have the children create a poster of things they can aim to do to avoid temptation. On the poster have them glue pictures or write descriptions of what Jesus did, such as read scriptures, pray, fast, or spend time in nature. Ask, what things does Satan like to tempt people to do? What can we do to follow Jesus's example and avoid temptation?

21. Water Turned to Wine

The first miracle of the Savior's ministry was turning water into wine at a wedding in Cana of Galilee. During the wedding the wine ran out and Jesus's mother petitioned Him to help. Jesus told the servants to fill six large stone waterpots with water. After the stone pots were filled to the brim, Jesus turned the water to wine and instructed the servants to take some to the governor of the feast. Those who drank of the miraculous wine remarked at its good quality.

Discussion Questions:

1. Jesus seemed reluctant to perform this miracle, saying, "Mine hour is not yet come" (John 2:4). What do you think He meant by this statement? Why would performing the miracle be too soon?

2. In your opinion, why might John have included this miracle in his Gospel? What is its significance? What can we learn from it?

3. What is your impression of Jesus's relationship with His mother, Mary, in this story? What example does Jesus set for parent and adult children relationships?

For Children:

Place a few drops of red food coloring into the bottom of a clear, but empty, glass. Use your hand to prevent others from seeing the dye in the glass. Fill a second clear glass up with warm water. Share the story of the miracle of the water being turned into wine. When the Savior performs the miracle, pour the warm water into the glass with the drops of red dye. After finishing the story, ask, why do you think this miracle is included in the Bible? What do we learn about Jesus?

22. Capernaum

Capernaum was a small fishing village located on the northwest shore of the Sea of Galilee during the life of Christ. It was the hometown of Matthew the publican. Jesus made Capernaum His home during the years of His ministry: "And leaving Nazareth, he came and dwelt in Capernaum" (Matt 4:13). Jesus preached in the synagogue there; He also performed several miracles in Capernaum, including the healing of Peter's mother-in-law and a man raised down through the roof.

Discussion Questions:

1. While Jesus was in Capernaum, He called a number of his disciples. How do you think Jesus chose the disciples? Is this process still used to choose apostles today?

2. Capernaum was the backdrop of many of Christ's mighty miracles. What would you think if miracles of healing and being raised from the dead were occurring in your hometown? How do you think the people of Capernaum reacted to Jesus?

3. Most of the people of Capernaum heard and saw what Jesus did and said, but they refused to believe (John 1:12; 12:42). Why do many who learn about the Savior choose not to follow Him? What reasons do they give?

For Children:

Use building blocks or other toys to make a pretend city of Capernaum. Be sure to include a synagogue, magistrate office, marketplace, tavern, inn, a pier, fishing boats, homes of the apostles, etc. Explain that at the start of Jesus's ministry He moved from Galilee to Capernaum. Here Jesus called at least five of the 12 disciples, including Peter, Andrew, James, John, and Matthew. Ask, how do you think Jesus chose the disciples? Is this process still used to choose apostles today?

23. Nicodemus

Nicodemus was "a ruler of the Jews" (John 3:1) and a member of the Sanhedrin, a Jewish religious body that ruled Jews within the Roman empire. Nicodemus came to see Jesus in the night, asking how the miracles he'd witnessed could be performed without the help of God. Despite his questions, Nicodemus treats the Savior with respect, calling him rabbi and a prophet. In response, the Savior taught Nicodemus about the importance of being born again.

Discussion Questions:

1. How would you define the phrase "born again" in your own words? How are we spiritually reborn through Christ?

2. Why might John have included Nicodemus in his writings? What can we learn from Nicodemus's story?

3. As Christ teaches Nicodemus, we read John 3:16—one of the most famous verses in the Bible. What does this verse mean to you? How does reading this verse in its original context help you appreciate it even more?

For Children:

After reviewing the story of Nicodemus visiting the Savior at night, use an object lesson to teach the importance of being born again. Use a permanent marker to write on a white board. Compare the marks to sin. Explain that no matter how much we might want to get rid of our sins, we can't do that on our own. We need the help of the Savior. To be born again means we believe in the Atonement of Jesus Christ and are willing to put our faith in Him and repent. Color over the permanent marker with a dry erase marker, then wipe it away (will also remove the permanent marks). Ask, why do you think Jesus told Nicodemus he needed to be born again? How can we be born again?

24. Samaritan Woman at the Well

Near the beginning of Jesus's ministry, He traveled into Samaria and stopped at Jacob's Well, waiting while his disciples went to a nearby town to purchase food. While there, Jesus encountered a Samaritan woman who came to get water around noonday. When He asked the woman for a drink, she wondered why a Jew would accept water from her. Jesus engaged her in conversation. He offered her living water, prophetically revealed details of her life, and affirmed His identity as the Messiah.

Discussion Questions:

1. Jesus's conversation with this woman is unexpected because of her gender, nationality, and past. Why does Jesus hold the conversation with the Samaritan woman? Why her?

2. The Savior starts a conversation with the woman by asking for a drink of water. What is your best conversation starter with strangers? How do you bring up gospel subjects?

3. After feeling the Spirit and learning Jesus's true identity, the woman hastens back to town to tell others. What would you have done if you were the Samaritan woman? Who would you tell first?

For Children:

Take your family to visit a well or spring of water. While there, share the story of Jesus's conversation with the Samaritan woman at the well. In feeling the Spirit and learning Jesus's true identity, the woman hastens back to town to tell others. Ask, what would you have done if you were the Samaritan woman? Who would you tell first?

25. Sermon on the Mount

The Sermon on the Mount is the most famous speech given by Jesus Christ during His earthly ministry. Found in Matthew 5-7, the sermon established foundational guidelines for Christian behavior as Jesus asked His followers to live a higher law. The opening section of the sermon, often called the Beatitudes, is particularly well-known. Jesus delivered the same sermon, with slight changes, to people in the Book of Mormon.

Discussion Questions:

1. In the Beatitudes, Jesus uses the term *blessed* numerous times. What does this term mean? How might the world interpret *blessed* differently than the Savior intended?

2. In the Sermon on the Mount, Jesus is essentially telling the people that they will no longer need to live the Law of Moses. How might this change have been difficult for the Jews? What changes in the Church have been hard for you to make or adapt to?

3. According to Jesus, the merciful will be shown mercy. Why is it so hard to show mercy to people who have wronged us? How can we develop this Christlike quality?

For Children:

Play seek and find using artist Harry Anderson's painting Sermon on the Mount. See if the children can locate the following items in the painting: a pot, sailboat, satchel, purple hat, yellow flowers, boulder. After, share the story of Jesus giving the Sermon on the Mount. Explain that this famous sermon explained Christianity and Christian behavior to the people. Read some of the sermon in Matthew 5. Ask, what part did you like best? Why? What did Jesus teach in that passage?

26. Blind Man in Bethsaida

While Jesus was in Bethsaida, a blind man was brought to Him to be healed. The Savior "spit on his eyes" and blessed the blind man. At first the blind man still did not see clearly, saying, "I see men as trees, walking." Jesus then touched the man's eyes, and soon his sight was restored. The Savior sent the man home, telling him not to go into town or to tell anyone in town about his being healed (Mark 8:22-26).

Discussion Questions:

1. Why did the Savior treat this blind man differently than others He had healed? What are we supposed to learn or recognize from this miracle?

2. Jesus seems to be teaching his disciples as much as He is healing the blind man. What does it mean to be spiritually blind? How can we be healed from spiritual blindness?

3. Jesus has to touch the man twice to fully heal him. Have you ever had an answer to prayer, but at some point needed a "second touch?" What happened?

For Children:

Blindfold family members and provide each person with a piece of paper and a pencil. Instruct each person to try and draw a picture of a tree. After each person is done, look at the pictures and discuss how hard it is to draw without being able to see. Share the miracle of the blind man in Bethsaida being healed. Ask, what do you think life was like for the blind man before he was healed? How might this miracle have changed the man's life?

27. Pool of Siloam

The Pool of Siloam was the location where Jesus healed a blind man. Located south of Jerusalem's Temple Mount, the freshwater pool was likely used for ritual bathing. The Siloam Pool was fed by waters from the Gihon Spring, located in the Kidron Valley. In the Old Testament, King Hezekiah had the Siloam Tunnel dug underneath Jerusalem to bring water from the spring, outside the city wall. The Siloam Pool is where those making an annual pilgrimage to the temple would start before ascending to the inner temple court to make sacrificial offerings.

Discussion Questions:

1. According to John 9:7, Siloam means sent. Why do you think John includes this detail in the telling of the healing of the blind man from birth? Who was sent, Jesus or the blind man?

2. The Pool of Siloam was located close to the temple. When the Savior sent the blind man to wash there, was Jesus also inferring the man should go to the temple? Why or why not?

3. The Pool of Siloam was used for ritual bathing, a location known today as a mikveh. Have you ever seen or visited a mikveh? Why do you think ritual cleansing like this is not a part of most Christian churches? Should it be? Why or why not?

For Children:

Take your children swimming. At the pool, pretend the water is the Pool of Siloam. Share the story of Jesus sending the blind man to wash his eyes in the Pool of Siloam. Explain that the pool, often used for ritual cleansing, was located near the temple. Ask, do you think Jesus was telling the blind man to go to the temple when he sent him to the Pool of Siloam? Why might Jesus want him to go to the temple?

28. Centurion's Servant Healed

While in Capernaum, a Centurion approached Jesus and asked Him to heal a servant who suffered from palsy. The Savior offered to go and heal the servant, but the Centurion felt too unworthy as a Roman soldier to have the Lord in his home and told Jesus, "But speak the word only, and my servant shall be healed" (Matt. 8:8). Marveling at the Centurion, Jesus responded, "So be it done," and the servant was healed that hour (Matt. 8:13).

Discussion Questions:

1. Jesus told the Centurion, "I have not found so great faith, no, not in Israel" (Matt. 8:10). Does this surprise you? Why or why not? What kind of faith was Jesus talking about?

2. How did this Centurion show his faith? How can we follow the Centurion's example in our own faith? Share a time you had to exercise your faith through action?

3. How would you define faith? Which scriptural definition of faith do you like best? How much faith does a person need to possess to be healed? How much faith do we need to have the Lord hear our prayers?

For Children:

Let the children practice using adhesive bandages on each other, making an arm sling out of a bandana, or using crutches. Tell a story about a time when you were sick. After, share the miracle of when Jesus healed the Centurion's servant. Ask, how did this Centurion show his faith? How can we follow the Centurion's example in our own faith?

29. Daughter of Jairus

Jairus, a ruler from a synagogue, approached Jesus. Falling at the Savior's feet, Jairus implored Him to come heal his dying 12-year-old daughter. On the way to Jairus's home, a messenger arrived, saying the girl had died. Jesus continued to Jairus's home anyway. When they arrived at the house Jesus told the mourners that the girl was not dead, but asleep. Taking only the parents and three of his disciples into the girl's room, Jesus took the daughter by the hand and commanded her to arise. Immediately, she rose from her bed and was healed.

Discussion Questions:

1. Jairus asked Jesus to "come and lay hands" on his daughter (Mark 5:23). What does this reveal about Jairus's knowledge of the priesthood? What does it say about his faith in Christ?

2. Why do you think the Savior limited the number of disciples who came with Him to Jairus's home? Why do you think Jesus only allowed the parents, Peter, James and John in the girl's room?

3. What is the connection between faith and fear in this miracle? How can we overcome our fears to exercise greater faith?

For Children:

As a family, play a game of Sleeping Lions. All but one player is a "lion." The lions lie down on the floor, eyes closed, as if they were sleeping. The "hunter" moves about the room attempting to encourage the lions to move by getting close to them, telling jokes, or doing silly things. Any person who moves must stand up and join in the hunt. The game continues until the last lion moves. After playing, tell the story of Jairus's daughter being raised from the dead. Ask, why do you think Jesus said the daughter was only sleeping? How do you think the parents felt when their daughter was healed?

30. Healing at Pool of Bethesda

Jesus came to a pool in Jerusalem called Bethesda, a gathering location for many with disabilities and illnesses. They gathered at Bethesda because they believed a tradition that said every so often an angel would stir the waters of the pool, and the first person to step in would be healed. When Jesus came, He spoke to a man who had been waiting at Bethesda for many years, hoping to be healed; but the man had never been able to get to the water first. Jesus had compassion on the man and healed him by saying, "Rise, take up thy bed, and walk" (John 5:8).

Discussion Questions:

1. Why did Jesus only heal the one man at the Pool of Bethesda when many others in need were also there? Was He unloving? Why might the Savior leave us in our trials?

2. Why did Jesus ask the man if he wanted to be healed? Do you think the man wanted to be healed? Why or why not? What reasons do people have for not wanting to be healed by the Savior?

3. Jesus healed this disabled man on the Sabbath and was criticized by Jewish leaders for doing so. What standards can we use to determine what behaviors help us to keep the Sabbath day holy?

For Children:

Play some favorite water games with your children (i.e., swimming pool games, water balloon fight, or running through sprinklers). Share the story of the man waiting by the Pool of Bethesda being healed by Jesus. Emphasize that Jesus only healed the one man when there were others there who had disabilities and were sick. Ask, why do you think Jesus only healed the one man at the Pool of Bethesda when many others in need were also there? How do trials help us to grow?

31. Bleeding Woman Heal

A woman who had suffered for over ten years with "an issue of blood" (Mark 5:25) had faith enough to reach out and touch the hem of Jesus's robe while He walked through a crowd of people. When she reached out, Jesus immediately felt His healing power had been accessed and asked who had touched Him. The woman came and knelt before Him in fear, but told what she had done. In response the Savior said, "Daughter, thy faith hath made thee whole" (Mark 5:34).

Discussion Questions:

1. What do you learn from this story? If we are intentional in our faith, will God heal us of our physical ailments? Why or why not? Why might some be left unhealed, despite their faith in the Savior?

2. Jesus told the woman her faith had made her whole. What is the relationship between the power of faith and the power of the priesthood? How might the priesthood power have been involved in the woman's healing?

3. Why do you think this woman's illness was healed? What do you think she learned from her experience? Was her testimony of the Savior changed by the miracle? Why or why not?

For Children:

Fill a bag or pillowcase with different objects or various sizes and textures. Remind the children that God has blessed us with different senses, including sight, hearing, touch, etc. Let each child reach into the bag and feel the objects. After everyone has reached in, have them guess what they felt. Share the story of the bleeding woman healed by touching Jesus. After, ask, how do you think Jesus knew he had been touched? Why do you think this woman's illness was healed? What do you think she learned from her experience?

32. Widow of Nain

The Widow of Nain is an unnamed woman mentioned by Luke. She lived in the village of Nain, located only seven miles from the Lord's hometown of Nazareth. When Jesus came across a funeral procession in Nain, He seemed to immediately recognize the woman and understood that the funeral was for her son. Whether or not He knew the Widow of Nain personally, Jesus did know that within a few years His own mother would lose a Son. "Weep not," the Savior told her (Luke 7:13), then He touched the man and raised him from the dead.

Discussion Questions:

1. The Savior often shows special concern for mothers, like the Widow of Nain. Why do you think the Savior has compassion for mothers? How can we improve our care and respect for mothers around us?

2. Luke gives only a sparse description of the Widow of Nain; she is both nameless and voiceless. Do you think Luke's lack of description was purposeful? Why or why not? How are widows voiceless and nameless in today's society?

3. The miracle granted to the Widow of Nain seems to foreshadow the resurrection. What parallels do you see in the two events?

For Children:

Play charades using the following mom actions: pretend to be . . . mom cooking dinner; mom folding the laundry; mom doing something she likes; mom when she's happy; mom when she's angry; mom getting ready for church. After, tell the children the story of the Widow of Nain and her son being raised from the dead. Ask, why do you think the Savior loves mothers? What can we do to show love and care for mothers?

33. Calling of the Apostles

As Jesus began His ministry, He invited individuals to follow Him. Soon many were coming to the Savior to be healed, and the small group of those who followed and traveled with Him was growing. One day Jesus went up onto a mountain and invited specific followers to come with Him. While on the mountain 12 were ordained to be Apostles of the Lord, including Simon Peter, James, John, Andrew, Philip, Bartholomew, Matthew, Thomas, James, Thaddaeus, Simon, and Judas.

Discussion Questions:

1. Why did Jesus go up on a mountain to ordain the apostles? Why was it not done in a public setting? In your opinion, why are setting-apart blessings usually done in a private location?

2. What do you know about the original 12 apostles? Which of the original 12 apostles would you most like to meet? Why?

3. What authority did Jesus confer on His Apostles? What were they supposed to do with this authority or power? How is this similar to latter-day apostles?

For Children:

Show your children pictures of the latter-day apostles currently serving in the Church. Explain that these men are ordained apostles called to serve the Lord and to be witnesses of Christ. Share the story of Jesus calling and ordaining 12 Apostles on the mountain. If possible, show a picture of Jesus's 12 original disciples and review their names. Ask, how did these men witness of Christ? What have latter-day apostles done to witness of Christ?

34. Matthew (Levi)

Matthew, typically believed to be Levi, was a publican (tax collector) for the Romans when he was bid by Jesus to follow and become on of His disciples. "As a Jew, Matthew saw Christianity as the culmination of Judaism, with Jesus as the promised Messiah" (Phillips, Wm. Revell. "Matthew, Gospel of." *Encyclopedia of Mormonism*, New York: Macmillan Publishing Company, 1992, 869). Because of this, Matthew provides a genealogy of the Savior at the beginning of his book and often includes stories demonstrating the fulfillment of Old Testament prophecies.

Discussion Questions:

1. As a tax collector for the Romans, Matthew was probably not well liked by his people. What impact would being called as a disciple of Christ have had on Matthew's life? How might he have been treated differently?

2. Matthew records that Jesus wants His followers to be a light to the world. How can we be a light to others? Share a time when you were able to be a light to someone. What happened?

3. Matthew provides a genealogy of the Savior's Davidic (royal) line, proving his right to reign. Why do you think this genealogy was ignored by the Jews? What do you learn about Jesus from the genealogy?

For Children:

Gather family members together in a darkened room. Discuss why some are afraid of the dark or why it is hard to do things in the dark. Turn on a flashlight and point out that, although there is still much of the room in shadow, the light helps us see. Explain that Jesus wants us to be a light to the world. Ask, how can we be a light to others? When have you been a light to someone? How does being a light to others help them?

35. James the Great

The most well-known James in the New Testament was one of Christ's original 12 apostles. James and John are both identified as sons of Zebedee. The Savior Himself surnamed James and his brother John as Boanerges, or "sons of thunder" (Mark 3:14-17). This James served with Peter and John in what could be described as the First Presidency of the Church in ancient times; he was present with the Savior and these great men on the Mount of Transfiguration and in the Garden of Gethsemane. James is the only apostle whose martyrdom is confirmed in the New Testament. He died when Herod Agrippa I had him beheaded (Acts 12:1-2).

Discussion Questions:

1. Why do you think the Lord gave James and John the surname Boanerges ("sons of thunder")? What personal characteristics could this have referred to?

2. James was a witness to some of the most important spiritual events of all history. If you could speak with him face to face, what questions would you ask him about these events? Why?

3. What do you think are the biggest differences in serving in the First Presidency in James's day versus our current day? What similarities do you see?

For Children:

Show the children photographs of the current First Presidency of the Church and take time to learn their names and a little about them. Explain that God uses presidencies, or presiding councils, to help lead and guide the Church. This practice was first used by Jesus when Peter, James, and John were called to preside over the Church in the days following the Savior's ministry. Ask, what do you think it was like being an apostle in Jesus's time? What challenges did apostles have then and now?

36. Parable of the Sower

In this parable a farmer goes to sow, or plant, seeds. While planting, some of the seeds fall to the wayside and get eaten by birds. Next, the farmer drops some of the seeds on a stony patch of ground where there was only a little soil for growth; when the seeds were sprouted and the sun got hot, they died because the roots were too shallow. Some other seeds fell among thorny weeds and the sprouts died because the weeds crowded them out. Finally, some seeds fell into good ground, sprouted, and eventually brought forth varying amounts of fruit (Matt. 13:3-9).

Discussion Questions:

1. The Savior mentions four types of soil, each resulting in different outcomes for the seeds. What do you think the soil represents? How can we place ourselves in soil that will help our testimony to grow?

2. Why do you think this parable is called the Parable of the Sower? Brainstorm other titles that could be used. What other names might be better for it?

3. In the story, Jesus implies that His teaching is like seeds. What do you think Jesus expects to happen in response to his teaching?

For Children:

Place some soil and dirt in plastic cups. You may choose to find a variety of soils as an experiment. Have the children plant some beans in the cups. Add water and sunlight. Read the Parable of the Sower and discuss the different types of soil. Explain that the seed is like a testimony that grows. Ask, how will the different types of soil influence the growth of our seeds? What things might help or harm the growth of seeds or a testimony?

37. Parable of the Wheat and Tares

In this parable the owner of a farm planted wheat in his fields, but during the night an enemy came and sowed tares (weeds) in with the wheat. When the field was sprouted and the blades began to show, the servants of the man recognized the weeds in among the wheat. The servants went and asked if the seed had been bad, but the owner realized his enemy had sabotaged the field and counseled the servants not to try and pull out the weeds "lest while ye gather up the tares, ye root up also the wheat with them." At harvest time the owner would have the reapers separate out, bundle, and burn the tares (Matt. 13:24-30).

Discussion Questions:

1. What is your immediate reaction to this parable? What emotion does it evoke? Why?

2. The Savior warns against pulling the tares (weeds) too soon because the wheat might be pulled up with them. Why is it often important to wait and withhold judgment when people do bad things?

3. A tare is a kind of weed that looks like wheat when it is a young plant. What is the Savior trying to compare tares to in this parable? What might the wheat represent?

For Children:

Buy two types of a treat that your children enjoy: one brand name and the other off brand. Remove any wrappings or packaging and offer the treat to your children. Do a taste test and ask if they can tell which of the treats are the brand name kind. After, tell the children that sometimes things that look similar are actually quite different. Share the Parable of the Wheat and Tares, then ask, how were the servants supposed to tell the difference between the wheat and tares (weeds)? Why is it often important to be patient people who make poor choices?

38. Parable of the Mustard Seed

In this parable the Savior makes a comparison between the kingdom of heaven and a grain of mustard seed. A man plants a tiny mustard seed in his field. Although the size of the seed was very small, the plant that grew from it eventually became a tree and "the greatest among herbs." The tree was large enough for birds to place their nests in its branches (Matt. 13:31–32).

Discussion Questions:

1. Besides comparing the mustard seed to the Kingdom of God, Joseph Smith compared it to the Book of Mormon. How is the Book of Mormon like a mustard seed?

2. What small steps have you taken to draw closer to God in your life? What have been the results of these small steps? In your opinion, are smaller or larger steps more effective in helping us to draw closer to God? Explain.

3. Which prophets in the scriptures or in latter-days could be compared to a mustard seed? Who else do you know whose faith might be comparable to a mustard seed? Explain.

For Children:

Have the children try dipping various finger foods (such as hot dog bites, soft pretzels, chicken nuggets, or tater tots) in mustard. Ask the children if they like it or not and why. Tell the children that mustard is made from the seeds of the mustard plant. Share the parable of the mustard seed with them, explaining that the seed of the mustard plant is extremely small. The Savior is telling us that small efforts to live the gospel can result in a lot of growth. Ask, what small steps can we take to live the gospel? What small steps can we make to get closer to Jesus and Heavenly Father?

39. Parable of the Hidden Treasure

In this pair of parables, Jesus first compares the kingdom of heaven to a treasure that is hidden in a field. When the treasure is found, the person who finds it sells all their belongings to be able to buy that field. Next, Jesus compares the kingdom of heaven to a sea merchant searching for pearls. When the sea merchant finds a particularly beautiful pearl, he goes and sells everything he owns to buy it (Matt. 13:44-46).

Discussion Questions:

1. What would be something temporal that worth selling all you had to obtain it? What would be something spiritual that would be of similar worth? In what ways are the values of temporal and spiritual things measured differently or similarly?

2. Who can you think of in the scriptures who sacrificed greatly to have the gospel in their lives? In your opinion, which person in scripture gave up or sacrificed the most?

3. What do you treasure most in your life right now? How did you obtain that treasure to begin with? What would you do if you lost that treasure?

For Children:

Ask the children to each show the family their three greatest treasures. Have them explain what they love and treasure about each item. After, share the Parable of the Hidden Treasure. Ask, what do you think Jesus was trying to compare the treasure or the pearl to? How valuable is having a testimony of the Jesus and His teachings?

40. Mary Magdalene

Mary Magdalene was one of the primary witnesses of the Resurrection of the Savior. She came from a small city on the Sea of Galilee, but became a disciple of Christ, following Him throughout much of His ministry. In the New Testament, Mary Magdalene is first introduced when Christ heals her of seven demons; she is often mentioned as being present during other significant events in the Savior's life. She stood by Mary, Jesus's mother, during the Crucifixion, and was the first person to arrive at the empty tomb and to see the resurrected Savior in the garden.

Discussion Questions:

1. When most of the 12 disciples had abandoned the Savior, why do you think Mary Magdalene chose to be present at Christ's death? What does this say about her as a person?

2. Mary demonstrated her love and devotion to the Savior in basic and practical ways. What are some practical ways we can show love for Jesus?

3. Like the disciples on the road to Emmaus, Mary does not initially recognize the Savior by the garden tomb. Why do you think this is? How might this be related to the Savior's resurrected state?

For Children:

Print out a copy of a picture of Mary Magdalene seeing the Resurrected Savior in the garden. Cut the picture up into puzzle pieces. Have the children take turns putting the puzzle together. Explain that the woman is Mary Magdalene, one of the Lord's disciples and followers. Mary showed her devotion to the Savior by cooking for the disciples, standing by Jesus during the crucifixion, and helping Jesus's mother. Ask, what are some practical ways we can show love for Jesus? Make a plan to follow through on one of the ideas discussed.

41. Simon Peter

Simon Peter was one of the original twelve disciples chosen by Jesus Christ. Peter (whose name means rock) became the leading disciple, belonging to Christ's inner circle. These three, Peter, James, and John, accompanied Christ at the resurrection of Jairus's daughter, on the Mount of Transfiguration, and in the Garden of Gethsemane. During his time with Christ, Peter tried to walk on water, but had to be rescued when he sank. After the Savior's resurrection, Peter became the head of the Church on the earth. He received the revelation that enabled the gospel to be taught to the Gentiles (Acts 10-11).

Discussion Questions:

1. The Savior told Peter to cast the nets on the opposite side of the boat to catch fish. What do you think Peter's reaction was like when the nets were full to overflowing? Have you ever been surprised by an overabundance of blessings from the Lord? What happened?

2. How did Simon Peter's background as a fisherman enable him to be an effective missionary? How does the Lord use your talents and strengths to help others?

3. Peter, despite being a faithful and obedient believer, is well-known for denying the Christ three times. Why do you think Peter denied Christ? What are some reasons that he did the very thing he said he would not do?

For Children:

Teach the children how to draw a simple picture of a sailboat. After the children have practiced a little, add to one of the pictures to illustrate the story of the time when Peter tried to walk on water and the Savior had to rescue him. Share the story with the children, then ask, why do you think Peter wanted to walk on the water? Why do you think he began to sink? How can we stay focused on Jesus when we are struggling?

42. Simon Peter's Catch

After a full night of failing to catch any fish, Simon Peter came to shore to wash out his net. Jesus asked permission to come aboard to teach the people on the shore from Simon's boat. After teaching, Jesus told Simon to take his boat out to deeper water and cast the net out again. Simon explained his failed night of fishing, then followed the Lord's instructions and let the net down. Soon the net had caught so many fish it began to break. His fishing partners came in a different boat to help with the haul, which filled both ships so full they began to sink.

Discussion Questions:

1. Simon has a failed night of fishing, but with Christ's help he sees success. When have you had success by involving the Lord in your efforts? How can we involve the Lord more fully in our daily lives?

2. Simon Peter was likely tired from being up all night and feeling defeated from his failed fishing trip. Why did he trust the Savior, whom he had just met? Why was he willing to do as Jesus asked?

3. Why did Jesus go on the boat to preach? How might this have influenced Simon Peter?

For Children:

Help your children learn about different types of fish people like to eat, such as cod, salmon, trout, etc. Find out what they look like, where they live, and how fishermen today catch them. Share the miracle of Simon Peter's catch of fish. Ask, why did Simon Peter trust Jesus enough to let his net down again? How do you think Simon felt when he saw all the fish in the net?

43. Five Loaves and Two Fishes

After learning the death of His cousin John the Baptist, Jesus went out into the desert to mourn. But when the people learned where He went, they followed to be taught and healed. When the day grew late the disciples said the people should be sent into the villages to get food to eat. But Jesus told the disciples to feed them. The disciples said, "We have here but five loaves, and two fishes" (Matt. 14:17). Jesus prayed over the bread and fish, tore it into pieces and gave it to the disciples to pass around the multitude. After everyone ate and was full, there were still 12 baskets full of food. About 5,000 people had been fed.

Discussion Questions:

1. Other than the resurrection of Jesus, this is the only miracle that is recorded in all four of the gospels. What makes this miracle so important in the life of Christ? What are we supposed to learn from it?

2. Have you ever faced an impossible situation where you felt completely unable to accomplish the task before you? What did you do and how did you get through it? What role did the Savior play?

3. Why do you think Jesus thanked God before sharing the food? What is the value of praying over food before a meal?

For Children:

Prepare a meal that includes both bread and fish. After blessing the food, share the miracle of the five loaves and two fishes with the children. Ask, why do you think Jesus thanked God before sharing the food? Why do we pray over the food before eating it?

44. Jesus Walks on Water

Jesus's disciples were on a ship when the weather turned bad, and they were caught in rough water. Late in the night the Savior came walking on the water toward the ship. At first the disciples feared Jesus was a spirit, but the Lord called to them, saying, "Be of good cheer; it is I; be not afraid" (Matt. 14:27). Peter tried to walk toward Jesus on the water; at first, Peter was able to do so, but began to sink when the wind and waves distracted his attention. The Savior grabbed ahold of Peter and told him not to doubt.

Discussion Questions:

1. Why did Jesus send the disciples on the ship knowing there would be a storm? How have the storms in your life served as teaching or learning opportunities?

2. If you were Peter, do you think you would have tried walking on the water to get to Jesus? Why or why not? What could walking on water be compared to in your life?

3. After Jesus got into the boat, the storm ceased. How has inviting Jesus into your boat helped you weather the storms of life?

For Children:

Play with toy boats in a child's pool or other large container. (Note: if you don't have a toy boat, consider folding paper sailboats.) Teach your children some of the parts of a boat, including, helm, rudder, sail, bow, and stern. Tell the children the miracle of Jesus walking on water, noting that after Jesus got in the boat the storm ceased. Ask, why was Jesus able to walk on the water and calm the storm? How can we eliminate our fears and trust Jesus more?

45. Sea of Galilee

The Sea of Galilee is the lowest freshwater lake in the world. It is located near a region named Galilee in northeast Israel. It is also known as the Sea of Tiberias and Sea of Kinneret, both names of cities located on the lake shores. In the New Testament, much of Jesus Christ's early ministry took place near of the Sea of Galilee; for example, the Sermon on the Mount was given on a hill overlooking the Sea of Kinneret. And Jesus calmed the storm and walked on the water there.

Discussion Questions:

1. Twice in the New Testament Jesus calms a storm while on the Sea of Galilee. Who do you know who weathers the storms of life really well? How does their faith play into that?

2. Jesus taught the crowds by the shore and preached while standing in a boat on the Sea of Galilee. Why would Jesus stand on a boat instead of preaching from the shore? Where does Jesus teach from today?

3. The Sea of Galilee is a freshwater lake that brings life to a desert region. How might the Sea of Galilee have inspired the Savior's comments on "living water" (John 4:10) to the woman at the well?

For Children:

Use Cub Scout Raingutter Regatta boat kits to make sail boats. Test the boats on a swimming pool or local lake. Tell the children about the Sea of Galilee being a lake in Israel where Jesus spent much of His time during His ministry on earth. Explain that sometimes Jesus would preach from a boat to large crowds on the shore of Galilee. Ask, why would Jesus stand on a boat instead of preaching from the shore? Where does Jesus teach us from today?

46. Jesus Calms the Storm

Jesus and the disciples were sailing across the Sea of Galilee when a storm overtook the ship. The waves began to crash onto them, scaring the disciples. Jesus was asleep, but the disciples woke Him because they were afraid and thought they were going to die. In response, Jesus said, "Why are ye fearful, O ye of little faith? Then he arose, and rebuked the winds and the sea; and there was a great calm" (Matt. 8:23-26).

Discussion Questions:

1. How was Jesus able to sleep through the storm? What does His lack of worry indicate? What implication does this story have for your storms and trials?

2. After the Lord calmed the storm the disciples marveled and said, "What manner of man is this, that even the winds and the sea obey him!" (Matt. 8:27). After all the disciples had witnessed, why did they marvel? What were they still learning about Jesus?

3. What role does fear currently play in your life? What are you most afraid of? How can having faith in Christ help you manage these fears?

For Children:

Create the sounds of a rainstorm with your hands using snaps, claps, and thunder made with feet stomping. Make an audio recording to play back, allowing the children to hear. After, tell the miracle of when Jesus calmed the storm while on a boat. Ask, how was Jesus able to sleep through the storm? Why were the disciples so fearful? What is the difference between faith and fear?

47. Mount of Transfiguration

Mount Tabor is thought to be the location of the Mount of Transfiguration. During this sacred event, apostles Peter, James, and John witnessed as the Savior spoke to Moses and Elijah, both translated beings. Then, they watched as a physical change came over the Savior and He appeared in a glorified and transfigured state. Moses and Elijah gave Peter, James, and John the priesthood keys needed to lead the Church and the apostles themselves were temporarily transfigured.

Discussion Questions:

1. John testified of the experience on the Mount of Transfiguration: "We beheld his glory, the glory as of the only begotten of the Father" (John 1:14). What do you think John meant? What does glory look like?

2. The transfiguration of the Savior occurred only a few months before the Savior's Atonement. How might the transfiguration have helped the Savior prepare for that challenging event?

3. Why is it significant that Moses and Elijah were present at this event? What do you think these translated men looked like?

For Children:

Let the children play dress-up using Halloween costumes or other dress-up items around the house. Explain that dressing up is a way to pretend we look like someone or something else. The word transfiguration is a word that means a person is changed to look glorious, like God. Review the story of Jesus, Peter, James, and John on the Mount of Transfiguration. Ask, how do you think this experience might have impacted the disciples? When has feeling the spirit impacted you? What happened?

48. Mount Tabor

Mount Tabor is located in the southern part of Galilee. It is a small mountain that rises abruptly from its surrounding plain. The height of Mount Tabor offers strategic control over a junction of two important trade routes through the area. In the Old Testament, it was the site of Israel's triumph over the Canaanite leader Sisera, which was prophesied of and led by the prophetess Deborah. In the New Testament Mount Tabor is the location more commonly known as the Mount of Transfiguration.

Discussion Questions:

1. Few events in the Bible are as important as what occurred on the Mount of Transfiguration. What can we learn from this sacred event? What similar events in the latter-days could be comparable to what occurred on Mount Tabor?

2. The Savior asks us to be "changed," or transfigured, by the Spirit of the Lord (2 Cor. 3:18). How does the Spirit change or transfigure us? What do you think it feels like?

3. What symbolism can you see in Mount Tabor's location, formation, and geography? Why might Jesus have chosen Mount Tabor for the location of His transfiguration?

For Children:

Use face paints or make-up to "transform" the children's faces into fun or dramatic new looks. Tell the story of Jesus and apostles Peter, James, and John going to Mount Tabor, hearing the voice of God, and witnessing the transfiguration of the Savior. Explain that transfiguration means Jesus appeared like a glorified and divine being, and that Jesus hopes someday we will all be changed and glorified too. Ask, how does following Jesus change us? What does it feel like to become more like Jesus?

49. Caesarea Philippi

Caesarea Philippi was an ancient Roman city known for pagan worship. It was located southwest of Mount Hermon and was considered Gentile territory. A cave there, known as the Gates of Hell, was viewed as a gate to the underworld and known for being a place of iniquity. The city is mentioned in both the Gospels of Matthew and Mark. While near the city, the Savior asked the disciples who they thought He was, to which Peter replied, "Thou art the Christ, the Son of the living God" (Mark 16:16). A woman from Caesarea Philippi, who had been bleeding for 12 years, was miraculously cured by Jesus.

Discussion Questions:

1. Caesarea Philippi was considered Gentile territory. Why do you think the Savior did not preach to the Gentiles during His earthly ministry?

2. At Caesarea Philippi the Savior states, "I say also unto thee, That thou art Peter, and upon this rock I will build my church; and the gates of hell shall not prevail against it" (Matt. 16:18). Considering the Gates of Hell cave, what object lesson is the Savior trying to teach?

3. Why do you think the Lord asked the disciples who He was? What was He trying to teach or learn?

For Children:

Sing the children's song "Going on a Bear Hunt" (lyrics found at allnurseryrhymes.com) together, including the verse about the deep, dark cave. After, share the story of Jesus and the disciples visiting Caesarea Philippi, where there was a cave known as the Gates of Hell. There the Savior said, "I say also unto thee, That thou art Peter, and upon this rock I will build my church; and the gates of hell shall not prevail against it" (Matt. 16:18). Ask, what is scary about deep, dark caves? How is a cave like hell? Why did Jesus teach that the Church would win against the gates of hell?

50. Samaria

Samaria was an area centrally located in Israel during the life of the Savior. It spread from the Jordan River on the east to the Mediterranean Ocean on the west, between Judea and Galilee. Despite having a similar religious and political heritage as the Jews, there was great tension between the two peoples because the Samaritans were considered to have sinned by marrying outside of the faith and accepting false teachings during the time when the Jews were held captive in Assyria and Babylon. The Savior showed love for and interacted with Samaritans; after His resurrection He directed the gospel be preached in Samaria.

Discussion Questions:

1. Who might be the "Samaritans" of the world today? Who is considered an outsider or unacceptable by the groups you belong to? Why? How should we treat them?

2. The Jews were willing to travel many miles out of the way to avoid Samaria. Why is avoiding interaction with those different than ourselves often ill-advised? What is the end result?

3. What can we learn from the Savior's interaction with the Samaritan woman at the well and the parable of the Good Samaritan? How would you describe the example set by the Savior?

For Children:

Print out a simple map of Israel and use a marker to outline Samaria (from the Jordan River on the east to the Mediterranean Ocean on the west, between Judea and Galilee). Explain that the Samaritans were considered to have sinned by marrying outside of the faith and accepting false teachings during the time when the Jews were held captive in Babylon. Still, Jesus treated them with love and respect. Ask, who do you know who is considered to be an outsider or not good enough? How would Jesus want us to treat people who are different than ourselves?

51. Parable of the Good Samaritan

A lawyer, in an effort to tempt Jesus, asked, "Who is my neighbor?" (Luke 10:29). In response, the Savior shared the Parable of the Good Samaritan. In the parable a man is traveling from Jerusalem to Jericho, but he is attacked and robbed along the way. Left to die on the side of the road, a priest and Levite both passed by the traveler without offering assistance. Finally, a Samaritan stopped to help. Despite being despised by the Jews, the Samaritan tended the traveler's wounds, and took him to an inn. After caring for the traveler overnight, the Samaritan left, but first arranged with the innkeeper to pay for the traveler's care. The parable implies that even strangers should be considered as neighbors.

Discussion Questions:

1. How does the Parable of the Good Samaritan answer the lawyer's question of "Who is my neighbor?" (Luke 10:29)? After reading the parable, how would you answer the lawyer?

2. The individuals in the parable seem to be of different ethnic backgrounds. Why do you think race or ethnicity is such a barrier to giving service to others? How can we overcome this barrier?

3. Which of the four types of service acts that the Good Samaritan performs is hardest for you personally (giving compassion, caring for physical needs, spending time in

service, or donating money)? Which is the easiest? Explain.

For Children:

Together, read the account of the Parable of the Good Samaritan in the September 2011 Liahona (p. 68; available on the Church website for free). Ask, how does Jesus's Parable of the Good Samaritan answer the lawyer's question of "Who is my neighbor?" (Luke 10:29). Which of our neighbors Jesus would want us to reach out and help? Make a plan to give service to a neighbor.

52. Jericho

Jericho is located west of the river Jordan and north of the Dead Sea. It is the lowest city in the world but has plenty of fresh spring water. When the 12 Tribes of Israel first entered into the land of Canaan by crossing the river Jordan, they did so near the city of Jericho, and a miraculous battle took place. In the New Testament, Jesus and the disciples passed through Jericho; here the Savior healed two blind beggars. The Savior used the road between Jerusalem and Jericho as inspiration for the Parable of the Good Samaritan.

Discussion Questions:

1. The two blind beggars recognized Jesus, saying, "Have mercy on us, O Lord, thou Son of David" (Matt. 20:30). Why do some recognize Jesus's power and divinity, but others seem blind to it? How can we learn to recognize the Savior's presence in our lives more fully?

2. Because of irrigation, Jericho was a fertile land known as the City of Palms; it also has some of the world's oldest protective walls. How might these traits of Jericho be symbolic of the Savior?

3. What similarities are there between life and the long, dangerous road from Jerusalem to Jericho? What was the Lord trying to teach us with the Parable of the Good Samaritan?

For Children:

Teach your children a basic hand clap game, such as Patty Cake, Miss Sue, or Miss Mary Mack (if needed there are videos online with instructions). After the children learn one well, have them try to do it with their eyes closed. Explain that blindness can make even simple games more challenging. Share the story of the Savior healing two blind men in Jericho. Ask, why do you think the blind men recognized Jesus and called out to Him? How can we learn to recognize Jesus's influence in our lives?

53. Mary and Martha

Mary and Martha were sisters who, along with their brother Lazarus, were beloved friends of the Savior. Jesus frequently visited their home during the last year of His ministry. During one visit He was accompanied by some of his disciples. Mary sat at the feet of the Savior learning from Him during the visit. Martha, however, wanted to be of service and sought to offer the visitors hospitality. In giving the service Martha became impatient and asked the Savior to have Mary help her. Jesus replied that Mary "hath chosen that good part, which shall not be taken away from her" (Luke 10:42).

Discussion Questions:

1. Jesus tells Martha to seek for "the good part" (Luke 10:42). In your opinion, what is "the good part" (Luke 10:42) mentioned by Jesus? How do we choose it?

2. What was Jesus referring to when He said it would "not be taken away" from Mary (Luke 10:42)? Why is it so valuable?

3. Martha seems to love being in the service of the Lord and her family. How do you feel about service? What blessings have you received from serving others?

For Children:

Invite a friend over for dinner or a play date. Before they arrive, explain the concept of hospitality and how to treat a guest well. Have the children help plan a snack or clean the house in preparation. Tell the story of Mary and Martha when Jesus visited their home. Ask, what is "the good part" (Luke 10:42)? How do we choose it?

54. Healing of Blind Man Since Birth

One Sabbath, Jesus, walking with the disciples, noticed a man who had been blind from birth. The disciples asked who had sinned: the man or his parents? Jesus told them neither had sinned, "but that the works of God should be made manifest in him" (John 9:3). Then, Jesus made clay, anointed the blind man's eyes, and told him to go wash in the Pool of Siloam. When the man did so, his eyes were healed. Many of the man's acquaintances were surprised to see he had been healed.

Discussion Questions:

1. Why did the disciples think the man's blindness had been caused by sin? Why do people still mistakenly assume a person's bad circumstances are caused by their own sin? How can we avoid this mindset?

2. This seems to be a two-part miracle: the anointing and the washing. Why did this miracle take two parts while others only need one?

3. The blind man's eyes were anointed and washed. How might this be symbolic of temple washing and anointing? What other parts of the miracle are related to the temple?

For Children:

Play "eye doctor" by making a vision test chart using letters or shapes in varying sizes on a large piece of paper. See how far away the children can stand and still read the chart. Have them try to describe the letters with only one eye open. After, share the miracle of Jesus healing the blind man from birth. Ask, why did the disciples think the man's blindness had been caused by sin? What is the real reason some people have disabilities or trials in their life?

55. Parable of the Lost Sheep

After the Pharisees and scribes criticized Jesus for meeting and eating with sinners, Jesus responded with a parable about a shepherd with a flock of 100 sheep. When the shepherd realized one of his lambs was missing, he went into the mountains to try and find it. After he found the lamb, he carried it home on his shoulders and rejoiced over it, even more than the 99 sheep that had not strayed. Jesus noted, "It is not the will of your Father which is in heaven, that one of these little ones should perish" (Matt. 18:11-14).

Discussion Questions:

1. This parable was given as part of a sermon on how to treat those who offend us. What point is the Savior trying to make? What do you learn from this parable?

2. Have you ever had a season where you felt lost or had gospel questions? How did you find answers or clarity? How did the Savior help in that process?

3. How can we support or show love to those who are spiritually or otherwise lost? How can we help celebrate or rejoice when someone returns to the fold or is found?

For Children:

Print a maze of the parable of the lost sheep from the internet (search images for maze of parable of lost sheep). Share the parable and have the children complete the maze. Discuss what the parable teaches about the Savior rescuing the lost sheep. Explain that, like the lost sheep, sometimes people stray from Jesus by sinning; but Jesus still loves those who stray and seeks to help them repent. Ask, how can we show love to those who are lost? How can we help celebrate or rejoice when someone returns to the fold?

56. Parable of the Foolish Rich Man

Jesus told a parable about a rich man whose crops were plentiful one year. The rich man decided to pull down his small barns so he could build larger storage for all the yield of the crops. The rich man thought that because he would have plenty of food laid up for many years, he would be able to "eat, drink, and be merry." But God took the rich man's soul that night and the man's stored food was for naught. Jesus warned, "So is he that layeth up treasure for himself, and is not rich toward God" (Luke 12:16-21).

Discussion Questions:

1. This parable was given after someone asked the Savior to speak to his brother about dividing an inheritance with him. How does this parable answer the question asked of Jesus? What might the person asking the question have thought?

2. When you have extra time, money, or resources, what do you tend to spend them on? What guidance has the Savior or prophets given about the use of overabundance?

3. What does it mean to be "rich toward God" (Luke 12:21)? How can we follow the Savior's counsel to be "rich toward God"?

For Children:

Teach children the value of money by either (for younger children) playing pretend store, or (for older children) having them go to a real store with a shopping list and a budget. After, share the Parable of the Foolish Rich Man and discuss how the rich man earned his wealth because of plentiful harvests made possible by the Lord. Explain that the rich man was being selfish with his riches. Ask, why is it important to share our time and money with those in need? What are some good ways to donate money and time?

57. Parable of the Prodigal Son

A certain man had two sons. The younger son demanded his inheritance early, then left to live riotously in the city. After wasting all of the inheritance and realizing what he had lost, the son returned home and asked to be a servant to his father. But the father rejoiced in seeing the return of his son and celebrated with music and a feast. When the older son, who had dutifully served his father, came home to the celebration, he was angered. The father told his older son not to be angry, that he would inherit all.

Discussion Questions:

1. The Parable of the Prodigal Son was given after Pharisees complained about Jesus eating with sinners. What is Jesus trying to say to the Pharisees in response?

2. What gospel principles do you think the Parable of the Prodigal Son teaches us? What does it mean to you? How can we apply this parable to modern day situations?

3. The parable says that after losing all of his money the younger son "came to himself" (Luke 15:17). What does it mean to come to yourself? Share a time when you came to your senses about something. What happened?

For Children:

Watch the video Parable of the Prodigal Son, one of the Church's Bible videos (available to watch on the Church website or on YouTube; 5:34 min. length). After, ask, what was Jesus trying to teach when He gave this parable? Why did the father celebrate the return of his younger son?

58. Parable of the Lost Coin

The Savior told of a woman who had ten pieces of silver, but accidentally lost one in her home. The woman lit a candle and swept the whole house, looking diligently for the coin. After she finally found it, she called her neighbors over to celebrate with her, telling them, "Rejoice with me; for I have found the piece which I had lost." Jesus said that, like this woman, "There is joy in the presence of the angels of God over one sinner that repenteth" (Luke 15:8-10).

Discussion Questions:

1. What makes this parable so universal? What similarities or differences do you see in this parable as compared to other parables about things that are lost (i.e., sheep, prodigal son)?

2. Have you ever lost something of value and later found it? What happened? What did you learn from that experience?

3. The woman in the parable had ten pieces of silver. What might this symbolize? How might it be related to tithing?

For Children:

Ask the children to each share a personal story about a time they lost something important to them. Share the Parable of the Lost Coin and discuss how the woman went about finding the coin. Emphasize that Jesus and angels celebrate when we repent and follow Him. Ask, why did the woman celebrate after she found her coin? Why do angels and the Savior celebrate when we repent? What does repentance mean?

59. Ten Lepers Healed

As Jesus was journeying, ten lepers saw Him from a distance and called for the Savior to have mercy on them. Jesus went to them and healed all ten of the lepers. As the cleansed lepers departed, one, a Samaritan, turned back and, after glorifying God, fell down at the Savior's feet to give thanks. In response, Jesus asked, "Were there not ten cleansed? but where are the nine?" Jesus then told the Samaritan man that his faith had made him whole (Luke 17:12-19).

Discussion Questions:

1. The lepers immediately call to Jesus when they see Him. Do you think they knew the Savior? Explain. How much faith did they have in Christ?

2. What excuses could the other nine have given for not returning and thanking Jesus? What excuses do people make today for not thanking God or others?

3. Besides being cured of leprosy, the Samaritan who returned received forgiveness for his sins. What is the relationship between gratitude and the Atonement?

For Children:

Ask your family to stand in a circle. Have the first person say one thing they are thankful for. Have the next person repeat the first and add a second. Continue around the circle until someone forgets one of the items given. After, share the story of the healing of the ten lepers. Ask, what excuses could the other nine have given for not returning and thanking Jesus? When and how should we show gratitude to the Savior?

60. Martha

Martha and her siblings, Mary and Lazarus, were beloved friends of the Savior. Over the course of three stories shared about Martha and her siblings, it is clear to see the growth of her faith in Christ. In particular, after the death of Lazarus, Martha greeted Jesus on His arrival and expressed confidence that He would have healed her brother. She also testified of the eventual resurrection. Because of Martha's faith, the Savior raised Lazarus from the dead.

Discussion Questions:

1. Christ doesn't return to help Mary and Martha's brother Lazarus until it is too late. Why does the Lord often make us wait for promised blessings? How can we learn to accept the Lord's timetable for our lives?

2. Martha does not complain that the Lord did not arrive in time to help her brother. What is the problem with murmuring or complaining? How can we curb the habit of complaining?

3. Martha's testimony of the Savior clearly grows over the stories shared in the scriptures. What progress can you see in the growth of your own faith? How do you measure the growth of your own faith?

For Children:

Share a personal story about a time when something you prayed for did not happen. Explain that sometimes the Lord has a different timetable or has planned different blessings altogether for us. Complaining about our circumstances shows a lack of faith in God. Share the story of Mary and Martha sending for Jesus to come and heal Lazarus. Point out that Martha did not complain that Jesus arrived too late. After, ask, what is the problem with murmuring or complaining? How can we learn not to complain so much?

61. Mary, Sister of Martha

Mary and her siblings, Martha and Lazarus, were beloved friends of the Savior. Mary demonstrated true discipleship in her willingness to sit at the feet of the Savior to hear His words. During Christ's visit, shortly before the crucifixion, Mary anointed the Savior's feet and head using an expensive oil. In doing so she showed her understanding of Christ's mission and His impending death. When Judas Iscariot criticized the expense of the oil that could be sold to help the poor, Jesus defended Mary's actions.

Discussion Questions:

1. The spikenard oil Mary used to anoint the Savior was very expensive. Why did Mary choose to use such a high-quality oil? Why should our gifts or contributions to the Lord be of the best quality?

2. What do you think Mary learned at the feet of Jesus? What do you think it would be like to sit at the feet of the Savior and hear Him teach?

3. Mary used her hair to wipe the oil from Jesus's feet. Why do you think she used her hair instead of a towel of some sort? What symbolism do you see in Mary's actions?

For Children:

Use some lotion or baby oil to rub on your children's feet. Discuss how the oil or lotion feels on their skin. Tell the story of Mary anointing the feet of the Savior with expensive spikenard oil. Ask, why did Mary choose to use such a high-quality oil? Why should our gifts or contributions to the Lord be of the best quality?

62. Lazarus

Lazarus and his sisters, Mary and Martha, were beloved friends of the Savior. When Lazarus became seriously ill his sisters sent word to Jesus that "he whom thou lovest is sick" (John 11:3). Jesus was about 25 miles away when He received the petition to return, but delayed leaving for two days. By the time Jesus arrived, Lazarus had been entombed for four days. Mary and Martha expressed faith in the Lord's ability to heal Lazarus and took Jesus to the tomb. There, the Savior called for Lazarus to come forth and he was raised from the dead.

Discussion Questions:

1. Mary and Martha asked for Lazarus to be healed, but received a greater miracle. Share a time the Lord gave you a greater blessing than you expected. What happened? Why do you think the Lord is sometimes extra generous in His blessings?

2. Why do you think the Savior purposefully waited to return and help Lazarus? What does the Lord want us to learn from this miraculous experience?

3. How does belief in Jesus change your perspective on life and death? What kind of hope do you have because of your belief in Jesus as the Son of God?

For Children:

Use a doll and a roll of toilet paper to show the children how those who died in ancient times were wrapped in a shroud, like a mummy. Tell the story of Lazarus's death and being raised by the Savior. Ask, if you were to see a man who had been dead for four days walk out of a tomb, how would you react? How do you think Mary and Martha felt?

63. Cursing the Fig Tree

While walking into Jerusalem, Jesus was hungry. Seeing a fig tree by the road, He went up to it to get some fruit to eat. The fig tree, however, was barren of fruit. In response Jesus told the fig tree, "Let no fruit grow on thee henceforward for ever" (Matt. 21:19). Within a short time, the fig tree withered and died. The disciples were surprised at the speed the fig tree died, but Jesus told them that a prayer of faith is answered.

Discussion Questions:

1. What should the fig tree have been doing? Was the tree doing what God wanted it to do? Why or why not? Why do you think Jesus cursed the fig tree?

2. In what way was Jesus's command to the fig tree a prayer? How was this prayer similar or different from more a traditional prayer format? Share a time you prayed with faith. What happened?

3. Sometimes the cursing of the fig tree is described as a parable. What might the cursing of the fig tree symbolize as a parable? What are we supposed to learn from the cursing of the fig tree?

For Children:

Try a recipe or food that has fig as an ingredient. If possible, have the children try a piece of fig itself. Ask the children if they like the taste of the fruit. Share the miracle of Jesus cursing the fig tree. Ask, was the tree doing what God wanted it to do? Why or why not? Why do you think Jesus cursed the fig tree?

64. Triumphal Entry

The Sunday prior to the Savior's death, He entered Jerusalem. Before entering the city, Jesus sent two of the disciples into town to borrow a colt. The disciples placed their coats on the back of the colt and Jesus rode it into Jerusalem to the temple. Many went before the Savior waving palm fronds and crying hosanna. The triumphal entry fulfilled Old Testament prophecy: "Behold, thy King cometh unto thee: he is just, and having salvation; lowly, and riding . . . upon a colt the foal of an ass" (Zech. 9:9).

Discussion Questions:

1. Hosanna means *save now*. What does Jesus save us from? What symbols of salvation were used during this event?

2. A false narrative is a false story or belief that we hold about something. What false narrative did the Jews have about Jesus that is evident in the triumphal entry? What false narratives do you see about Jesus today?

3. What thoughts or questions do you have about the Savior's triumphal entry? What do you think it would have been like to witness the triumphal entry?

For Children:

Trace the children's hands on a piece of paper. Color one handprint to look like a donkey (thumb is the head and fingers are the legs) and the other to look like a palm frond. Share the story of Jesus's triumphal entry into Jerusalem. Explain that waving palm fronds symbolizes victory and peace. After, ask, why do you think Jesus rode into the city on the back of a colt? Why did the people wave palm fronds? What victory did Jesus win?

65. Herod's Temple

King Herod I of Judea was responsible for rebuilding the temple in Jerusalem that was used while the Savior was on the earth. More than 15 years before Jesus was born King Herod began to restore and expand the temple. The work was still in progress when Christ was born and continued for more than 30 years after His death. By the time 12-year-old Jesus went to the temple much of it was already in use. During His ministry the Savior often taught in the temple. He also went there many other times to walk and be with the people. It was here that He used a whip to clear out the money changers (Matt. 21:12).

Discussion Questions:

1. Herod's temple seems to have played a central role in the lives of the Jews in Israel. How can we make the temple more central in our lives today?

2. Although the Ark of the Covenant and other artifacts were not in Herod's Temple, the Lord still called it "my Father's house" (John 2:16) and "my house" (Matt. 21:13). In your opinion, what makes a temple the house of the Lord?

3. The Savior's life is deeply tied to Herod's Temple. 3. Which of the stories of the Savior in the temple are meaningful to you? Explain.

For Children:

Take a field trip to the grounds of a nearby temple or look at pictures of temples online or in a book. Ask the children which features they like about the temple or the gardens they see. Explain that the Savior visited the temple in Jerusalem many times. Share some of the stories in the scriptures about the Savior in the temple. Ask, which of the stories of the Savior in the temple do you like the best? Why do you think Jesus spent a lot of time in the temple?

66. Jesus Cleanses the Temple

Near the beginning of His ministry Jesus went to Jerusalem for the Passover. There, He found oxen and sheep being sold by money changers in the temple. Jesus braided a whip to use to clear the temple of money changers. Jesus cast out all of the people buying and selling in the temple, saying, "It is written, My house shall be called the house of prayer; but ye have made it a den of thieves" (Matt. 21:13).

Discussion Questions:

1. What was wrong with providing a service for buying sacrificial animals and exchanging currency for people who were from out of town? What do you think was really going on in these transactions?

2. In your opinion, did Jesus get angry on this occasion? Was His behavior violent? Is anger an emotion that is sinful? Why or why not? How is anger best expressed?

3. After Jesus cleansed the temple, the disciples recall the words of Psalms 119:139: "My zeal hath consumed me, because mine enemies have forgotten thy words." Why are the disciples reminded of this verse? What could this verse apply to today?

For Children:

Jesus braided a whip to cleanse the temple. Teach your children how to braid using yarn or ribbon. Practice while listening to the story of Jesus cleansing the temple (John 2:13-17). After, ask, was Jesus angry when He cleansed the temple? Is getting angry a sin? How is anger best expressed?

67. Parable of the Two Sons

Jesus posed a parable for the chief priests and elders to consider. In the parable, a man with two sons asks his oldest son to work in his vineyard. The son initially says he won't, but then later repents and goes to work. Then the man asks his second son to work in the vineyard. The second son lies; he agrees to go, but never does. After sharing this parable, Jesus asked the chief priests and elders which of the sons had obeyed the father, to which they answered the first son. "Jesus saith unto them, Verily I say unto you, That the publicans and the harlots go into the kingdom of God before you" (Matt. 21:28-31).

Discussion Questions:

1. The chief priests and elders had asked Christ about His authority; His response in part included this parable. What does this story have to do with authority? What was being taught?

2. The first son in the parable refuses to go work, then changes his mind. Have you ever at first refused a calling or service opportunity, then changed your mind or regretted your decision? What happened?

3. In what ways are we invited to work in the Lord's vineyard? How can we foster a positive attitude for these opportunities?

For Children:

Invite the children to help with a large household chore, such as cleaning a room or working in the yard. While working, share the Parable of the Two Sons. Look for comparisons between the parable and the children's response to the request to help. Ask, how did you feel when you were asked to help? Why do you think the first son refused, then changed his mind?

68. Parable of the Ten Virgins

Ten virgins took their lamps with them as they waited for the Bridegroom. Half of the virgins were wise, half foolish. The foolish virgins didn't take extra oil for their lamps. They slumbered while they waited, but finally at midnight the Bridegroom approached. The virgins rose and trimmed their lamps, but those of the foolish virgins had run out of oil. The foolish virgins asked the others to share their oil, but the wise virgins told them to go and buy more. While they were gone the Bridegroom came and the door was shut. When the foolish virgins returned and tried to enter the wedding, the Bridegroom turned them away, saying, "I know you not" (Matt. 25:12).

Discussion Questions:

1. This parable was received after the Savior was asked when the Second Coming and end of the world would occur. What does the parable reveal about the Second Coming? What did you learn?

2. When the foolish virgins returned with their oil and tried to enter they were turned away by the Bridegroom. Why do you think the Bridegroom says, "I know you not" (Matt. 25:12)? How do we come to know the Bridegroom?

3. Who do you think the ten virgins represent? What makes them wise and foolish? How can we make sure we are in the group of the wise virgins?

For Children:

Have the children make their own middle Eastern lamps out of a paper plate or construction paper (find a pattern online). While making the lamps, share the Parable of the Ten Virgins. After, ask, who do you think the ten virgins represent? What makes them wise and foolish? How can we keep our lamps filled?

69. Parable of the Sheep and Goats

In this parable of the Second Coming the separation of nations is compared to a Shepherd that divides his sheep from the goats; the sheep will be put on his right hand, the goats on his left. The King will tell those on His right hand they have inherited the kingdom because they fed and cared for Him. Confused, the righteous ask when they performed this service. In response the King says, "Verily I say unto you, Inasmuch as ye have done it unto one of the least of these my brethren, ye have done it unto me" (Matt. 25:40). Those on His left hand will be cast out.

Discussion Questions:

1. This parable was received after the Savior was asked when the Second Coming and end of the world would occur. What does the parable reveal about the Second Coming? What did you learn?

2. What do we learn from this passage about important things we should be doing while waiting for the Savior's return? How can we find opportunities to give service more regularly?

3. What impressions do you have of sheep and goats? How are they different or similar? How does this affect your understanding of the parable?

For Children:

Share the Parable of the Sheep and Goats with the children. Remind them that in the parable the King says the righteous helped Him when He was hungry, thirsty, a stranger, naked, sick, and in prison. Have the children make up an action that goes along with each of these services (i.e., placing hands on the stomach for being hungry). Try to memorize Matthew 25:35-36 by repeating it several times together using the actions. Ask, why does Jesus want us to serve people with these needs? Who could we serve this week? Make a plan to give service.

70. Olivet Discourse

The Olivet Discourse is a sermon given by the Savior that is recorded in Matthew 24-25. The sermon was given on the Mount of Olives, shortly before Jesus's crucifixion, and is primarily about the Second Coming. The discourse begins when Jesus tells the disciples that the temple in Jerusalem will be destroyed and in response they ask when it will happen. Great clarification was given to the Olivet Discourse by Joseph Smith (see Joseph Smith-Matthew in the Pearl of Great Price).

Discussion Questions:

1. The Savior teaches in JS-M 1:22, "They shall deceive the very elect, who are the elect according to the covenant." What do you think it means to be "elect according to the covenant"? How can we protect ourselves from being deceived?

2. Jesus offers the brief parable about the gathering: "Behold, wheresoever the carcass is, there will the eagles be gathered together; so likewise shall mine elect be gathered from the four quarters of the earth" (JS-M 1:27). What do you think this means? What should we learn from it?

3. Jesus mentions the prophets Moses, Noah, and Daniel in the Olivet Discourse. What value do you think there is in studying the Old Testament for information about the Second Coming? Explain.

For Children:

Have your children solve the "Jesus Christ will Come Again" cryptogram found in the September 2001 *Friend* magazine (p. 27). Explain that the cryptogram message comes from one of Jesus's sermons called the Olivet Discourse, which talks about the signs of the Second Coming. After solving the cryptogram, ask, why do you think no one knows when the Second Coming will happen? How can we prepare for Jesus to come again?

71. Parable of the Budding Fig Tree

Jesus told a parable about a fig tree to help His disciples better understand how to watch for the Second Coming. When a fig tree is young, and just putting out leaves, we can tell that summer is near. Just like watching for leaves on a fig tree, when we see the signs the Savior talked about in the Olivet Discourse, then we can know the Second Coming is close. "This generation shall not pass, till all these things be fulfilled. Heaven and earth shall pass away, but my words shall not pass away" (Matt. 24:32-35).

Discussion Questions:

1. What plants or signs in nature do you use to recognize changes in seasons? In your opinion, why is the fig tree metaphor effective? Explain.

2. Which of all the signs of the Second Coming do you look for or keep in mind? What signs have you seen take place? What signs do you think will come soon?

3. Why is it that the Savior's words will not pass away? How will they be preserved and utilized in eternity? How can we ensure the Savior's words are written on our hearts?

For Children:

Go for a nature walk to look for signs of seasons and change. Point out leaves, flowers, insects, and weather patterns. Tell the children that signs in nature give us clues about what weather is coming and how far off seasonal changes may occur. Share the Parable of the Fig Tree with the children, explaining that watching for changes in nature is like watching for signs of when the Savior will come again. Ask, what are some signs the Savior has told us to watch for? Why does Jesus want us to watch for signs of His Second Coming?

72. Parable of the Talents

In the parable of the talents, a man preparing to go to a far country needs to leave his property in the watch care of his servants. Before departing, he places five talents with one servant, two talents with another, and one talent with a final servant. During the master's absence, the servant who was given five talents doubled the value through trade. The servant given two talents gained two others. But the servant given only one talent buried it. When the master returned, each servant gave an accounting. The two servants who doubled the value of their talents were praised, but the servant who hid his in the earth was chastised and the talent was given to the servant with ten.

Discussion Questions:

1. What kinds of things has God entrusted to us in this life? What does God expect us to do with the things we are entrusted with?

2. What does it mean to increase talents? How does a person double their talents, like the servants in the parable?

3. What are some ways you can use your gifts and talents to serve God? Who do you know who excels at using their talents to serve God? What do they do?

For Children:

Have each family member make a list of talents they see in each other. Share and discuss the lists with each other. Review the parable of the talents in Matthew 25. Ask, what are some ways you can use your gifts and talents to serve God? How can we increase our talents?

73. The Last Supper

The night before Jesus's crucifixion, Jesus and his disciples ate their Passover meal, the Last Supper, in an upper room in Jerusalem. In advance of the meal, Jesus sent two disciples to arrange accommodations in a room that was prepared. During the meal Jesus announced that one of the disciples would betray Him. The ordinance of the sacrament was introduced during the Last Supper; Jesus gave the disciples bread and wine to eat in remembrance of His body and blood. Jesus also took time to wash the feet of His disciples, demonstrating servant leadership.

Discussion Questions:

1. The Last Supper is described in four different books of the New Testament. Why do you think it is repeated so many times? What are we supposed to learn from it?

2. The sacrament ordinance was introduced at the Last Supper. Why do you think bread and wine were chosen to signify Jesus's body and blood? Why did Jesus want his disciples to use bread and wine to remember Him?

3. The Savior demonstrated servant leadership during the Last Supper. Who do you know who has been a good example of servant leadership? What was it like to have them as a leader?

For Children:

Write the events of The Last Supper on different word strips (Jesus sends disciples to find the room, Jesus announces one will betray Him, Jesus introduces the sacrament, Jesus washes the feet of the disciples). Tell the story of the Last Supper and have the children put the word strips in the correct order. Ask, what is the most important thing that happened at the Last Supper? How can we make taking the sacrament more meaningful?

74. Intercessory Prayer

An intercessor is someone who intercedes or pleads on behalf of another. During the Last Supper the Savior offered what is called the Intercessory Prayer, in which the Savior prayed to the Father on behalf of humankind. In the Intercessory Prayer, Jesus asked that the disciples be sanctified through the word of truth. He prayed for all those who believe in Him, that they would be united with the Godhead and be made perfect. The Intercessory Prayer recorded in John 17 is similar to that offered in 3 Nephi 19.

Discussion Questions:

1. How do you feel about the Savior praying for you specifically? What thoughts does this bring to mind? How does the Intercessory Prayer compare to prayers the Savior gave in Third Nephi while visiting the Americas?

2. Why did John record this prayer? What are we to learn about Jesus based on His prayer? What can we learn about prayer from this story?

3. The Savior prays that "they may be made perfect in one" (John 17:23). How does being unified help us to be made perfect? What other blessings come from being unified?

For Children:

Remind the children about a time your family prayed on behalf of someone in need. Explain that Jesus prayed on behalf of His disciples, as well as for us in the Intercessory Prayer. Read John 17:20-21 where Christ prayed for all those who believe in Him. Ask, how do you feel about the Savior praying for you? How can we be one with Jesus?

75. Judas Iscariot

Judas Iscariot was one of the original twelve disciples chosen by Jesus Christ and the only one not from Galilee. Judas is famous for betraying the Savior to the Sanhedrin for 30 pieces of silver; his name has become synonymous for being a traitor. At the Last Supper, Jesus predicted the betrayal. After the Lord's visit to Gethsemane that same evening, Judas arrived with Roman guards and signaled who Christ was with a kiss. This led to the arrest, trial, and crucifixion. Judas later attempted to return the money he had been paid, but he was unable to prevent Jesus's death. Recognizing his sin, Judas committed suicide by hanging himself from a tree.

Discussion Questions:

1. In your opinion, what is the most tragic part of Judas Iscariot's story? What lessons can we learn from Judas?

2. Do you think Judas's betrayal was necessary to set in motion the chain of events leading to the death and resurrection of the Savior? Why or why not? How might the Atonement have taken place without Judas's betrayal?

3. Do you think Jesus would have known from the beginning that Judas would betray Him? Why would Judas have been called as an Apostle if Christ knew beforehand?

For Children:

Read Chapter 52, "The Trials of Jesus", of the New Testament Stories for children (available on the Church website for free). Explain that Judas Iscariot was one of Jesus's disciples, but that he had betrayed the Lord. Ask, why do you think Judas was willing to betray Jesus for money? How do you think Judas felt after he betrayed Jesus?

76. Mount of Olives

Located on the eastern side of Jerusalem, the Mount of Olives is a prominent landmark in the life of Christ. The Mount of Olives is where Jesus delivered the Olivet Discourse. Jesus visited the Mount of Olives three times in the last week of His life, including going to the Garden of Gethsemane at the base of the Mount of Olives. The ascension of Christ occurred here. Several prophecies indicate the Mount of Olives will play an important role in the Second Coming.

Discussion Questions:

1. Why do you think the Lord went to the Mount of Olives so frequently? Where do you go when you need peace and solitude?

2. In the Olivet Discourse the Savior taught about the signs of the Second Coming. What signs of the Second Coming do you think are the most interesting? What signs are you watching for?

3. In 1841, Elder Orson Hyde dedicated the land of Palestine for the preaching of the restored gospel while on the Mount of Olives. Why do you think he chose this location? What significance does the Mount of Olives have to the Church today?

For Children:

Have the children taste test a variety of olives (either alone or in other dishes). Explain that olives grow on trees found in a dry, arid climate. Near Jerusalem there is a mountain ridge, which includes the Mount of Olives where olive trees are grown. Tell the children that the Mount of Olives is the location of the Garden of Gethsemane, where Jesus ascended into heaven, and where the Second Coming will occur. Ask, what do you think it will be like when Jesus comes again on the Mount of Olives? Would you like to be there? Why or why not?

77. Gethsemane

Gethsemane is a garden thought to be located somewhere at the base of the Mount of Olives. In Hebrew Gethsemane means *oil press*. On the last night of His life, the Savior went to Gethsemane with Peter, James, and John to pray. While praying, Jesus suffered great agony, taking on Himself the sins of the world. Luke said that during this time the Lord's "sweat was as it were great drops of blood" (Luke 22:44). This suffering, in combination with the crucifixion and resurrection, constitutes the Atonement. Shortly after, Jesus was arrested in Gethsemane by the Romans. Today, the exact location of Gethsemane is not known.

Discussion Questions:

1. Considering its importance, why do you think the exact location of the Garden of Gethsemane is not remembered? Why hasn't God revealed this?

2. Three key eternal events took places in gardens: the Garden of Eden, Garden of Gethsemane, and the Garden of Joseph of Arimathea's tomb. Why do you think this is? What is special about gardens?

3. What does Jesus's time in the Garden of Gethsemane teach us about His humanity? What does it teach us about His divinity?

For Children:

Visit a local garden and teach the children some of the plant names. Take some time in the garden to share the story of Jesus visiting the Garden of Gethsemane and praying in agony. Explain that this prayer was the beginning of Christ's Atonement. Ask, what do you think the Garden of Gethsemane might have been like that night? Why do you think Jesus decided to pray outside in a garden?

78. Sanhedrin

The Sanhedrin was a group of 71 Jewish leaders who sat in council as both a senate and a supreme court over the Jewish people, with the High Priest as the chief officer. Because of Roman rule, during the life of the Savior the Sanhedrin was restricted in its power to a jurisdiction of Judea proper. As a result, the Sanhedrin could not control Jesus because His ministry took place primarily outside of Judea; it wasn't until Jesus came to Jerusalem that they could arrest Him for blasphemy.

Discussion Questions:

1. Nicodemus was known to be a member of the Sanhedrin. How might his membership in the Sanhedrin have influenced his interaction with the Savior?

2. When Paul stood before the Sanhedrin, he told them he had fulfilled his duty to God in all good conscience (Acts 23:1). How do you think the Sanhedrin felt about Paul's change in allegiance?

3. Why do you think the Sanhedrin wanted to convict Jesus of a crime? Why did they feel threatened?

For Children:

Teach your children some Greek words, such as *polis* (city), *eros* (love), *logos* (logic), *eureka* (discovery), *phobia* (fear), and *yassas* (hello). Tell the children that two other Greek words, *sun* (with) and *hedra* (seat), were combined to form the name Sanhedrin, indicating they had seats of power. Teach the children that during Jesus's time the Sanhedrin was a group of Jewish religious leaders who would decide the rules people should follow and if someone needed to repent. Ask, why do you think the Sanhedrin leaders did not recognize Jesus as the Messiah?

79. Annas

Annas was a high priest appointed by the Roman governor Quirinius; Annas served in this position for ten years (from AD 6–16). Although he was retired at the time of Jesus's trial, Annas likely had great influence because the current high priest was his son-in-law, Caiaphas. The Gospel of John indicates Jesus was first taken to Annas for brief questioning before being sent to Caiaphas's home to be questioned by the Sanhedrin. Later, Annas presided over the trials of Peter and John before the Sanhedrin.

Discussion Questions:

1. The high priest Annas rejected the true High Priest Jesus. Why do you think Annas did not recognize the Savior? How might his position and authority have influenced Annas's choices?

2. Jesus tells Annas to question witnesses, those who have heard Him teach, or the apostles. What value is the witness of the apostles on the earth today? How has their witness influenced you?

3. Jesus refused to give specific answers to Annas's questions. Why do you think He did this? How would you respond if you were in a similar situation?

For Children:

Obtain a toy police badge and play cops and robbers with the children. After, tell the story of Annas questioning Jesus before the Sanhedrin trial. Explain that Annas was considered a high priest in the Jewish faith, but he had been appointed by the Romans—not by prophecy or someone with priesthood authority. Make a comparison to the toy police badge and the authority of a real badge. Ask, how did Annas behave when questioning Jesus? How would a real high priest, who represented Heavenly Father, have behaved when questioning Jesus?

80. Joseph ben Caiaphas

Joseph ben Caiaphas was one of the Jewish high priests who presided over the Sanhedrin trial of Jesus immediately before the crucifixion. Caiaphas had been made a high priest by the Romans and served in that position for 18 years. The meeting at which Jewish leaders plotted to kill Jesus was held in Caiaphas's home. During the trial, when Jesus proclaimed, "Hereafter shall ye see the Son of man sitting on the right hand of power, and coming in the clouds of heaven" (Matt 26:64), Caiaphas tore his clothes, declared Jesus to have blasphemed, and handed Him over to Pilate.

Discussion Questions:

1. Caiaphas was appointed high priest by the Romans. Why would the Jews allow the Romans to appoint their religious leaders? Why might Caiaphas have felt threatened by Jesus?

2. Caiaphas, the chief priests, and the Pharisees worried about losing their temple and their nation because of Jesus. What are some things you worry about losing by following Jesus or His commandments?

3. Jesus's ministry greatly challenged Caiaphas; he felt he was losing control. In what areas of your life do you feel in control of now? How would you feel if you no longer had that part of your life in control?

For Children:

Look up the painting Moses Gives Aaron the Priesthood in the Old Testament (Gospel Art Kit 108; available on the Church website). Point out that in the painting Aaron is shown wearing high priest clothing. Explain that Aaron was made the high priest by Moses, who had authority. He was set apart by the laying on of hands. Tell the story of Caiaphas being appointed as high priest by the Romans—who didn't have authority—during Jesus's time. Ask, how should high priests be chosen, by government leaders or by Church leaders with authority? How do you think Jesus felt about the high priest not having true authority?

81. Trials of Christ

As Jesus finished praying in the Garden of Gethsemane, Judas Iscariot arrived with a group of men. With a kiss on the cheek, Judas betrayed Christ. After being arrested, Jesus was taken to the high priest Caiaphas. The Jewish leaders found Jesus had blasphemed by claiming to be the Son of God; Jesus did not deny the accusation. Because the Jewish court did not have authority to sentence Jesus to death, they took Him to Pontius Pilate. Although Pilate did not think Jesus was guilty, the crowds cried out for Jesus to be crucified. Pilate washed his hands of the matter but gave the crowd permission to kill Jesus.

Discussion Questions:

1. Jesus was accused unfairly in His trial. Have you ever dealt with unfair accusations? What advice would you give someone who is dealing with unfair accusations in their life?

2. In the trial Pilate asks Jesus if He is King of the Jews. What do we mean today when we say Jesus is our Savior and King? How does this impact you personally?

3. In your opinion, why do you think Jesus kept quiet instead of defending Himself or witnessing to this group of people? What would you have done in that situation?

For Children:

Hold a mock trial over a simple dispute at home. Assign family members in the roles of lawyers, judge, and note taker. After the trial, discuss what helped make the mock trial fair or unfair. Explain that Jesus went through an unfair trial the night before He was crucified. Ask, have you ever dealt with unfair accusations? How do you think Jesus felt during the trial?

82. Procla (Pilate's Wife)

As Romans, Pontius Pilate and his wife, Procla, did not live in Jerusalem regularly. However, they were visiting the city when the vendetta against the Savior came to a head. Procla, apparently a woman of faith, had a dream about the Savior. Her dream made her so uncomfortable that she felt compelled to approach Pilate while he was in formal meetings on the chair of judgment. She explained her dream and recommended that her husband not let Jesus Christ be punished unjustly. Although Pilate did not follow his wife's advice, her interference on behalf of the Savior was recorded in scripture.

Discussion Questions:

1. Procla took great risk in speaking to her husband, interrupting Pilate during Jesus's trial. Why do you think she was willing to do so? How do you think Pilate might have felt about her interference?

2. Procla seems to have had different faith beliefs than her husband. How can we maintain relationships when our personal beliefs differ greatly from loved ones?

3. Since the Atonement had to take place, why do you think Procla was given her dream? What was the purpose of her dream?

For Children:

Explain that one of the ways Heavenly Father sometimes communicates with His children is through dreams. For example, Joseph was warned to take Mary and Jesus to Egypt in a dream; and Peter was given a dream that helped him to see the gospel could be taught to gentiles. Share the story of Procla, the wife of Pontius Pilate, having a dream and warning her husband about punishing Jesus. Ask, why do you think the Lord gave Procla the dream? How do you think she felt after having the dream about Jesus?

83. Pontius Pilate

Pontius Pilate was the Roman-appointed governor of Judea under Tiberius Caesar from A.D. 26–36; he presided over the trial of Jesus Christ and ordered the crucifixion. Prior to being the governor, Pilate was a military man. During his time as governor, he incurred enmity from the Jews by killing some of the them, having Roman troops encamped in Jerusalem, and trying to abolish Jewish laws. Although Pilate seemed to conclude Jesus was innocent, and his wife counseled him not to convict Jesus, the crowd of Jews swayed his decision.

Discussion Questions:

1. When you read the statements of Pilate, "Behold the man!" (John 19:5) and "Behold your King!" (John 19:14), what comes to your mind? In what ways are these titles correct and appropriate? In what way are they incorrect and inappropriate?

2. Pilate tries to appease the Jews by having Jesus scourged and beaten. Why would he be willing to do this when he believed Jesus to be innocent?

3. During the trial of Jesus Pilate asked the question, "What is truth?" (John 18:38). Why do you think Pilate asked this question? How would you answer him?

For Children:

Trace an outline on the sidewalk of each child's body using chalk. Be sure each tracing makes the children look like they are standing. Let the children add facial features, clothing, etc. Point out the standing positions of the chalk drawings and explain that sometimes it is important to stand up for and defend things we know to be good and true. Share the story of Pilate giving in to the Jews during the trial of Jesus. Ask, why do you think Pilate didn't stand up for Jesus? Why did he give in to the Jews?

84. Simon of Cyrene

After being arrested and tried, Jesus Christ suffered a brutal beating and public humiliation. He was so weakened afterward that carrying the cross became a burden His body struggled to bear. The Roman soldiers grew impatient with the Savior's slow progress under the weight of the cross and compelled Simon of Cyrene, who was coming into Jerusalem from the country, to carry the cross instead. Simon and at least two of his sons were early members of the Christian faith.

Discussion Questions:

1. The Gospel of Mark states that Simon was the father of Alexander and Rufus, who were early converts to the Church. How might the experience of carrying the cross have influenced the testimonies of Simon's family members?

2. Carrying the cross was a socially degrading burden forced on Simon. How do you think he felt during that time? In your opinion, what would be the worst part of the experience?

3. What is the likelihood Simon learned of the resurrection the following Sunday? What do you think was his reaction to all of these happenings, especially considering his unexpected involvement?

For Children:

Roleplay a bus accident with the children. Have them pretend they were passengers, the driver, or emergency responders helping on the scene. After, ask how they felt being helped or helping others. Share the story of Simon of Cyrene helping Jesus by carrying the cross. Ask, how do you think Simon felt helping carry the cross for Jesus? Why is it important to reach out and help those we see in need?

85. Jesus is Crucified

After being sentenced to death Jesus was mocked, beaten, then dressed in a purple robe and crown of thorns. Jesus was forced to carry the cross, but Simon the Cyrene was pulled from the crowd to carry it when Jesus moved too slowly. After His hands and feet were nailed to the cross, He was lifted up between two thieves. Jesus prayed on the cross and asked God to forgive those who harmed Him; He also spoke to His mother and to the apostle John. After many hours, Jesus died. At His death, an earthquake caused the earth to tremble and the veil of the temple was torn.

Discussion Questions:

1. Pilate placed a sign that read "King of the Jews" over Jesus's head. Why do you think Pilate did this? Was it done in cruelty or to point out the truth? Explain.

2. Why is it significant that Jesus was forsaken by the Father during the crucifixion? Share a time in your life you felt forsaken or distant from Heavenly Father. What happened?

3. What part of the Atonement do you think was likely the hardest for the Savior, the Garden of Gethsemane, the crucifixion, or going through the resurrection? What do you imagine each to be like?

For Children:

Read about the crucifixion in *New Testament Stories*, Chapter 53: Jesus is Crucified (available to read for free on the Church website). Explain that the crucifixion is part of the Atonement, Jesus's rescue mission to help us overcome sin and death. The Atonement enables us to return to live with Heavenly Father again. Ask, what part of the Atonement do you think was likely the hardest for the Savior, praying in the Garden of Gethsemane, the crucifixion, or going through the resurrection? What do you imagine each to be like?

86. Calvary

Calvary, also known as Golgotha or the place of the skull, is located just outside of Jerusalem's walls where Jesus Christ was crucified. Today the exact location of Calvary is not known, although in the book of Hebrews Calvary is described as being outside the gate (typically thought to be either Damascus Gate or Lions Gate). Whatever the location, Psalms 69:12 prophesies, "They that sit in the gate speak against me," indicating the place was likely within hearing distance of where Christ was crucified.

Discussion Questions:

1. Why do you think so many Christians focus on Jesus's crucifixion on Calvary instead of on the resurrection? Is it better to focus on one over the other? Why or why not?

2. Why would the Romans crucify people so close to the city gate? What purpose did that serve?

3. How do you think Jesus felt overhearing people speaking against Him as He was being crucified on their behalf? Share a time you overheard someone badmouthing you. How did you feel?

For Children:

Find and print a simple map of the gates around the city of Jerusalem (like the one by A to Z Kids Stuff). Share the map with the children and read off the different names of the gates. Explain that Calvary, the place where Jesus was crucified, was located just outside of the city wall, likely near Damascus Gate or Lions Gate. Ask, why do you think the Romans chose to crucify Jesus on Calvary? Why would they choose a place so near the city gates?

87. Joseph of Arimathea

Joseph of Arimathea was a member of the Sanhedrin, a Jewish religious body that ruled Jews within the Roman empire. According to the Talmud, he was the younger brother of the father of Mary, the mother of Jesus. Although limited information about Joseph of Arimathea is found in the New Testament, his journal has survived and is kept in the Vatican in Rome. As a wealthy man with political connections, Joseph used his influence to obtain possession of Christ's body after the Crucifixion; he wrapped the body in a clean linen cloth and placed it in his own garden tomb.

Discussion Questions:

1. Prior to the Savior's death it seems Joseph of Arimathea believed in the Savior, but he kept his faith private. In your opinion, is religious faith a public or private matter? Is it wrong to keep your religious beliefs private from co-workers or others?

2. Mark 15:43 states that Joseph "went in boldly unto Pilate." What personal risk do you think he was taking to do so? When have you had to live your faith boldly like Joseph?

3. Joseph of Arimathea placed the Savior in his own garden tomb. What possessions would you be willing to sacrifice for the Savior?

For Children:

Look at some headstones on findagrave.com or visit the grave of a family member or friend in a local cemetery. Explain that when a person dies the body is placed in a grave, where it will stay until the resurrection. Usually, graves are expensive. Tell the story of Joseph of Arimathea obtaining the body of the Savior after the crucifixion and placing it in his own tomb (type of grave). Ask, why do you think Joseph was willing to give Jesus his own tomb? What possessions would you be willing to sacrifice for the Savior?

88. Jesus is Resurrected

After Jesus's death on Friday, Joseph of Arimathea was given Jesus's body. Because the Sabbath (Saturday) was near, Joseph and Nicodemus hurriedly placed the body in a tomb and rolled a stone in front of the entrance. On Sunday morning, Mary Magdalene and other women went to the tomb but found it open and Jesus's body gone. They ran and told Peter and John, but the disciples didn't know what to do. Later, Mary saw the resurrected Savior near the tomb. Jesus sent her to tell His disciples He'd been resurrected.

Discussion Questions:

1. Jesus appeared to many people, both individuals and groups, after His resurrection. Which appearance is your favorite? Why?

2. When did the reality of the resurrection of Christ first impact you? What are your feelings about the resurrection?

3. How does your belief in the resurrection impact your feelings when someone you love dies? How is your outlook on life different from those who don't believe in the resurrection?

For Children:

Have a simple Easter egg hunt in a room of your home. After, ask the children why Easter is celebrated. Share the story of the resurrection of the Savior and some of the times Jesus appeared to people shortly after the resurrection. Remind the children that the resurrection is part of the Atonement. Ask, how does Jesus's resurrection help us? What part of the resurrection story is your favorite?

89. Joanna

Very little is known about Joanna, other than she was the wife of Chuza, the steward of Herod. Luke lists Joanna as one of a group of women who "had been healed of evil spirits and infirmities" and "ministered unto [Christ] of their substance" (Luke 8:2-3). Joanna was one of the women who went with Mary to anoint the Savior's body, but found the tomb empty. She became one of the witnesses of the resurrection.

Discussion Questions:

1. In Hebrew Joanna means *God has been gracious*. In what ways did Joanna serve graciously? In what ways was the Lord gracious with Joanna?

2. As one of the women who traveled with Jesus to help secure lodging, cook food, and take care of day-to-day needs, Joanna helped to support the work of the Lord. How can we follow Joanna's example in supporting the work? In what ways are cooking, cleaning, and completing household tasks helping to support the work of the Lord?

3. Joanna was a woman of means and influence. How do you think Joanna's husband felt about her giving financial support to Jesus? What should married couples do when they don't agree on financial issues?

For Children:

Get a transparent jar or container and some decorative rocks. Explain to the children that every time they say kind or gracious words about others it helps others feel good inside. Add a rock to the container when someone uses gracious words about another person. Share the story of Joanna in the Bible, helping Jesus by providing for day-to-day needs so He could continue to teach and minister. Explain that in Hebrew Joanna means *God has been gracious*. In what ways did Joanna serve graciously? How can we follow Joanna's example?

90. Thomas

Thomas, also called Didymus (twin), was one of the original twelve disciples chosen by Jesus Christ. When the other disciples were worried about the danger of traveling back to Judea, Thomas was willing to go when the Savior wanted to return after Lazarus fell ill and died. Thomas is often referred to as "doubting" because he did not believe the other disciples when they told him they had seen the resurrected Lord; however, later Thomas saw the Savior too and testified, "My Lord and my God" (John 20:28).

Discussion Questions:

1. Thomas asked Jesus to show the disciples the Father, to which Jesus famously responded, "I am the away, the truth, and the life: no man cometh unto the Father, but by me" (John 14:6). What can we learn from the Savior's response to Thomas?

2. When Jesus appeared to the disciples, Thomas was absent (John 20:24) and missed out. Why do you think the Lord prefers to appear to groups (see Matt. 18:20)? What things do we miss out on when we fail to attend our meetings?

3. The resurrected Savior said, "Thomas, because thou hast seen me, thou hast believed: blessed are they that have not seen, and yet have believed" (John 20:29). In what way are those who believe in, but haven't seen Jesus, blessed? How can we nurture our faith in Christ?

For Children:

Place a variety of items on a table and cover them with a tablecloth or blanket. Have the children try to identify various items based only on touch (through the tablecloth), sound, or smell. Explain that sometimes we figure things out without seeing them visually. Share the story of Thomas not believing that Jesus had appeared because he had not seen Him. Ask, how do you think you'd feel if Jesus came to our home? How can we know Jesus is here, even when we can't see Him?

91. Luke

The Gospel of Luke was written by a missionary companion of Paul. He appears to have been one of the early Gentile converts to Christianity. Luke and Paul journeyed together to Troas, Philippi, Jerusalem, and Rome. Luke was imprisoned with Paul while in Rome. Colossians 4:14 reveals that Luke was a physician. Luke's book is the longest of the four gospels detailing the life of Christ; the Book of Acts is considered to be a continuation of his writings. Legend has it Luke was martyred for his beliefs.

Discussion Questions:

1. Luke writes more about female characters of the time than any of the other authors of the Gospels. Why are these stories of faithful women important? Which is your favorite?

2. Luke likely wrote his Gospel after hearing stories of the Savior second-hand. In your opinion, are Luke's writings more or less powerful because they are second-hand accounts? Explain your thoughts.

3. What do you think it was like for Luke working as a missionary after the death of the Savior? Why do you think he continued to share the gospel despite all the persecution he experienced?

For Children:

Look at Bible map 13: The Missionary Journeys of the Apostle Paul. Have the children locate Troas, Philippi, Jerusalem, and Rome. Explain that one of Paul's missionary companions was Luke, who was the author of the Gospel of Luke and the Book of Acts. Although Luke never met the Savior personally, while traveling as a missionary he collected first-hand accounts of the Savior's life and ministry. Later, he used these to write parts of the New Testament. Ask, why do you think Luke collected stories about Jesus? How do stories about Jesus help us?

92. Ascension

The Ascension of Jesus into heaven occurred 40 days after the resurrection. During these weeks, the Savior showed Himself to more than 500 people and taught the disciples how they would carry on in leading the Church. At the time of the Ascension the disciples and the Lord were on the Mount of Olives; Jesus was taken up to Heaven in a cloud. Immediately after, two angels appeared and testified that Jesus "shall so come in like manner as ye have seen him go into heaven" (Acts 1:11).

Discussion Questions:

1. Why is Jesus's Ascension into heaven a significant event? In what ways does the Ascension indicate the success of Jesus's earthly ministry?

2. Immediately before His Ascension, the Lord tells the disciples, "Ye shall be witnesses unto me . . . in the uttermost part of the earth" (Acts 1:8). What does it mean to be a witness of Christ? Who on earth today is considered a witness of Christ?

3. Why do you think the Ascension took place on the Mount of Olives? Why do you think the Second Coming will take place at this same location?

For Children:

Provide collage materials such as buttons, dried pasta, beans, scraps of fabric or ribbon, cotton balls, leaves, etc. Read the story of the Ascension in Acts 1:4-12. Have each of the children make a collage of what they think the Ascension may have looked like. Let each child take a turn explaining their picture. After, ask, why is Jesus's Ascension into heaven a significant event? How is Jesus's Ascension similar to a missionary finishing their mission and going home?

93. Pentecost

The Pentecost was an event that took place about ten days after Jesus's Ascension into heaven. The apostles, while meeting together to celebrate the Feast of Weeks, were suddenly filled with the Holy Ghost, as had been promised by the Savior. Initially, the disciples heard the sound of rushing wind; they then saw a bright light, like fire. "And they were all filled with the Holy Ghost, and began to speak with other tongues, as the Spirit gave them utterance" (Acts 2:4). In latter-days, at the dedication of the Kirtland Temple similar spiritual occurrences to the Pentecost took place.

Discussion Questions:

1. Why do you think the disciples hadn't had the Holy Ghost with them prior to the Pentecost? What do you think they would have preferred more: having Jesus back on the earth, or having the gift of the Holy Ghost? Explain.

2. What are the various ways that we see the Holy Spirit manifested during the Pentecost? What are some of the ways the Holy Ghost manifests Himself in your life?

3. At the Pentecost, the disciples spoke in tongues using over 12 different languages. How have you seen the gift of tongues manifested in the latter-days? Would you like to experience this gift of the spirit? Why or why not?

For Children:

Draw and cut out a white dove from cardstock paper or a paper plate. Attach orange, red, or yellow ribbon or yarn to the dove to represent fire. Read about the Pentecost in Acts 2:1-38 and explain that the dove represents the Holy Ghost and the flames the disciples saw at the Pentecost. Make a list together of all the ways the disciples experienced the Holy Ghost during the Pentecost. Ask, what are some of the ways we see the Holy Ghost working today? How does the Holy Ghost help you?

94. Matthias

Matthias was the disciple chosen to replace Judas Iscariot after his suicide. Matthias was the first disciple who was not called directly by Jesus Christ. Peter proposed Matthias and Joseph called Barsabbas be considered for the calling. After praying, the disciples cast lots and Matthias was chosen. Extrabiblical sources say Matthias served missions in Judea and in modern-day Georgia, where he was stoned to death. A marker at some Roman ruins in Georgia claims Matthias is buried at that site.

Discussion Questions:

1. Do you think the process used to call Matthias as a disciple of Christ was appropriate? Why or why not? Why do you think the process of casting lots was used?

2. Why do you think Peter, as the prophet, didn't pick a replacement himself? How does the calling of Matthias to be a disciple compare to the process of calling apostles in modern times?

3. What qualities do you think Matthias must have had to be chosen as the replacement disciple? What kind of personality characteristics should we develop as we strive to become disciples ourselves?

For Children:

Show your children a variety of optical illusion pictures. Compare these images to the worth of souls to demonstrate how our perspective changes when we see others as God sees them. Tell the story of the disciples praying to ask God who the new disciple should be; they recognized God would know better than they would. Ask, why was understanding the hearts of these men important? How can we try to look at others as God sees them?

95. Paul (Saul)

Paul of Tarsus, a Pharisee known as Saul before his conversion to the gospel of Jesus Christ, is one of the most well-known New Testament apostles. Prior to his conversion, Paul persecuted the Church and even approved of Stephen's stoning. But on a trip to Damascus Paul had a vision of the Savior and was converted. After this vision Paul dedicated himself to the service of the Lord and became a powerful missionary. Several letters Paul wrote as an apostle are included in the New Testament and were referenced by Joseph Smith in a number of the Articles of Faith.

Discussion Questions:

1. In his vision of the Savior, Christ says to Paul, "It is hard for thee to kick against the pricks" (Acts 9:5). What does it mean to kick against the pricks? Share a time you kicked against the pricks in your life.

2. How hard might it have been for the early Church members to believe and accept Paul's conversion? What would your reaction be if someone so against the Church today had such a miraculous conversion?

3. Paul writes in Romans 1:16, "For I am not ashamed of the gospel of Christ." Why are some people ashamed of the gospel in their lives? How can we move beyond feeling ashamed and develop a deeper faith in Christ?

For Children:

Watch the Bible video "Paul: A Chosen Vessel" about the preparation and calling of Paul (available on the Church website). After, ask what was your favorite part of the story of Paul's conversion? Why did the Lord call Paul to be His servant and an apostle?

96. Saul's Conversion

A Pharisee born in Tarsus, Saul lived in Jerusalem at the time of Jesus's ministry. After the resurrection of Jesus, Saul began to persecute Christians and witnessed the stoning of the apostle Stephen. While traveling on the road to Damascus, Saul saw a bright light and heard a voice say, "Saul, Saul, why persecutest thou me?" (Acts 9:4). Blinded by this event, Saul prayed to know what the Lord would have him do. After three days Ananias, a Christian, healed Saul and taught him the gospel.

Discussion Questions:

1. Why do you think Saul was so fervent in his persecution of Christianity? How was he able to overcome his feelings about Christianity so quickly?

2. Saul did not eat or drink during the three days of his blindness. What might this indicate? How might this have influenced the efficacy of his prayers?

3. Ananias was likely very surprised at the instruction to find and heal Saul. What is the most surprising or unexpected thing that has ever happened to you? What unexpected promptings have you received?

For Children:

The November 1999 *Friend* magazine has flannel board pictures that can be used to tell the story of Saul's conversion. Have the children color and cut out the figures. Tell the story of Saul hearing Christ's voice while on the road to Damascus. Have the children take turns retelling the story using the flannel board pictures. Ask, why do you think Saul hated Christians so much? What made Saul change his mind about Jesus?

97. Ananias

Ananias was a Christian disciple who was inspired by the Lord to seek out Saul, who had been blinded by a light from heaven. Ananias was told to "inquire in the house of Judas" (Acts 9:11) for Saul, who had been praying. Because Saul had been persecuting the Saints, Ananias was hesitant to follow this prompting; however, he went when the Lord told him Saul was a "chosen vessel" (Acts 9:15). After being healed by Ananias, Saul was baptized.

Discussion Questions:

1. Ananias was hesitant to follow the prompting to seek out Saul. Have you ever questioned when you have received a prompting from the Lord? Share a personal experience.

2. Like Ananias, have you ever tried to explain things to the Lord, even though He is omniscient? How can we overcome the tendency to think we know more than God?

3. Ananias was told Saul was a "chosen vessel" (Acts 9:15). How do you interpret this phrase? Why do you think Saul was chosen when he had made such poor choices in his earlier life?

For Children:

Find a variety of cups, bowls, vases, or other "vessels" that can be filled with varied amounts of water. Let the children tap the vessels with a spoon or other utensil to make musical sounds. Explain that the containers of water could also be called vessels. After, tell the story of Ananias being told by the Lord to seek out Saul, a "chosen vessel" (Acts 9:15). Saul, later known as Paul, became a great leader and apostle. Ask, how did the Lord know Saul had such great potential? Why do you think Saul was chosen when he had made such poor choices?

98. Stephen

Stephen was "a man full of faith and of the Holy Ghost" (Acts 6:5) who was one of seven men chosen to help with the distribution of food to widows. Stephen performed miracles and boldly taught that the Law of Moses had been fulfilled in Christ. The Sanhedrin accused Stephen of blasphemy against Moses and God; during Stephen's trial they arranged for false witnesses to testify against him. Stephen became a martyr after being stoned to death.

Discussion Questions:

1. Besides Stephen, what other martyrs can you think of who died for Christ or the Church (both in the scriptures and in latter-days)? How can we honor the memory of those who were martyred for the gospel?

2. The last thing Stephen is recorded as saying before his death was, "Lord, lay not this sin to their charge" (Acts 7:60). Why do you think he forgave those who stoned him? How can we learn to forgive more readily?

3. What are some of Stephen's attributes that are Christlike? Which of these attributes would you most like to develop? Why?

For Children:

Watch the Church Bible video "The Martyrdom of Stephen" (5:33 min.; available on YouTube and on the Church website). Explain that when someone dies for their beliefs, they are called a martyr. Ask, why do you think Stephen was willing to die for his testimony of Jesus? What other martyrs can you think of who died for Christ or the Church?

99. Philip

Philip was one of the original twelve disciples chosen by Jesus Christ and is from the same hometown as Peter and Andrew. Philip was a follower of John the Baptist until John indicated Jesus was the Lamb of God. It was Philip who first introduced Nathanael to the Savior. Philip is mentioned most often in the Gospel of St. John. He asks the Savior how they should feed the 5000; and Philip served as a liaison when some Greek pilgrims are seeking Jesus in Jerusalem. Later, Philip served as a missionary in Samaria, Greece, Syria, and Turkey.

Discussion Questions:

1. Philip does not seem to understand the doctrine of the Godhead in John 14. How would you summarize the doctrine of the Godhead? Why is this information important for us to understand?

2. Jesus tells Philip, "If ye had known me, ye should have known my Father also" (John 14:7). What are some of the ways in which Jesus and Heavenly Father are the same? In what ways are they different?

3. In Acts 8 Philip is directed by an angel to Gaza, where Philip meets and shares the gospel with an Ethiopian eunuch reading Isaiah. What can we learn from Philip about following promptings to share the gospel?

For Children:

Teach your children the following action rhyme: "I pray to my Heavenly Father [fold arms]. I follow Jesus by choosing the right [walk in place]. The Holy Ghost can comfort me and help me feel warm and light [wrap arms around yourself in a hug]" (*Friend* magazine, April 2018). Explain that many people are confused by the differences between God, Jesus, and the Holy Ghost; even the disciple Philip misunderstood, but Jesus helped to teach Philip this doctrine. Ask, why would understanding about the Godhead be important to know?

100. Tabitha

Tabitha was a disciple of Christ. As a resident of Joppa, Tabitha (Greek name of Dorcas) worked to serve the needy people in her town. As a result, she was loved by her community. When Tabitha got sick and died unexpectedly, she was greatly mourned. The disciples in Joppa sent for Peter to come. Peter arrived and saw first-hand the powerful influence Tabitha had had on those around her. Peter prayed and then commanded Tabitha to arise; she came back to life and was healed.

Discussion Questions:

1. Why did the disciples in Joppa send for Peter? Why did they not use their priesthood to help Tabitha themselves?

2. The text tells us that Tabitha/Dorcas was "full of good works and acts of almsdeeds" (Acts 9:36). What might have been her Church calling in the congregation in Joppa? What Church callings provide greater opportunities for service?

3. One of Peter's first acts in Joppa is to clear the room and pray. Why doesn't Peter enlist the prayers of the friends and family members? Why does he want to pray alone?

For Children:

Share the story of Tabitha being brought back to life by Peter. Ask, how do you think the people of Joppa felt when Tabitha was brought back to life? What do you think Tabitha did after she was healed? Challenge the children to spend a week doing secret especial service for one of your family members. Watch over them, be mindful of times they need help, offer comfort, and give service when appropriate.

101. Council at Jerusalem

The earliest converts to the Church were Jews, but after the Ascension, the gospel was taken to Samaria and many there accepted Christ as their Savior. The cultural differences between Jews and Samaritans led to two questions about the necessity of Gentile converts living the Law of Moses and following some traditionally Jewish customs, such as circumcision. The apostles and Church leaders held the Council at Jerusalem, as detailed in Acts 15, to settle the issues.

Discussion Questions:

1. The Council at Jerusalem came up with four rules that all Gentile Christians should follow to help promote peace in the Church. How does the Church Handbook of rules and guidelines help promote peace today? Share a time the handbook has influenced or guided you.

2. At the Council, Jesus's half-brother James stated, "My sentence is, that we trouble not them" (Acts 15:19), meaning not make it difficult for Gentile converts. How can we make joining the Church an easier process for converts today? What difficulties might current-day converts experience when joining the Church?

3. What is the value of holding councils to solve problems? How are councils used in the Church today?

For Children:

Hold a family council to decide where you should go to get a treat after your next FHE. Have each person give a suggestion. Explain that you want the family to come to a unanimous decision (that you want everyone to agree). Take time to debate the different desserts and gradually come to a consensus. After this exercise, tell the children about the Council at Jerusalem (Acts 15). Ask, what is the value of holding councils to solve problems? When everyone agrees, how does that help the group?

102. Rhoda

Rhoda was a young servant in the household of Mary, the mother of John Mark. During a time when Peter was imprisoned, a group of Saints gathered in Mary's home to pray on his behalf. Rhoda was present, and as a follower of Christ, participated in the prayers. Late that night a knock sounded at the door; Rhoda went to answer it. On hearing Peter's voice at the gate, Rhoda became so excited that she ran to tell the others their prayers had been answered, but she forgot to admit Peter. At first the Saints there did not believe when Rhoda said Peter was at the gate, but her words were soon proved accurate.

Discussion Questions:

1. Rhoda could hear Peter and recognize his voice, even though he was not visible to her. Which of the voices of prophets or apostles today would you recognize without seeing their faces? Which would you most want to show up at your front door? Why?

2. How does Rhoda's example encourage you to share your testimony and faith with others?

3. Why did those who had been praying for Peter's release not believe when their prayers had been answered? How can we increase our faith to more readily see answers to prayer?

For Children:

Use one of the "guess the sound" games available on YouTube to see if your children can identify what they are hearing. After, tell the story of Rhoda recognizing Peter's voice, even though she could not hear him. Ask, which of the voices of prophets or apostles today would you recognize without seeing their faces? Which would you most want to show up at your front door? Why?

103. Silas

Silas, also called Silvanus, was one of the apostle Paul's missionary companions in Antioch, Corinth, Philippi, and Thessalonica in about 50 A.D. He was also a Roman citizen. Peter describes him as "a faithful brother" (1 Peter 5:12). Along with Judas Barsabbas, Silas was sent from Jerusalem to accompany Paul and Barnabas to the church at Antioch, where they were to confirm the decision of the Jerusalem Council. While serving as a missionary, Silas experienced persecution and imprisonment. Silas is also thought to have been a co-author or scribe to Paul for the letters to the Thessalonians.

Discussion Questions:

1. Silas experienced great trials and tribulations, but still praised God. How can we remember to keep the faith when we experience trials? Share something you do to stay close to God during trials.

2. Silas used his talents to serve the Lord. What talents do you have that could be used to serve God? What talents do your friends or family have that they use?

3. Paul and Silas were good friends to each other. In your opinion, what makes a good friend? Share what you appreciate most about one or two of your closest friends.

For Children:

Teach your children the song "Friends are Fun" (CS p. 262). When the children have learned the lyrics, ask what does the song say about being a good friend? Share the story of Paul and Silas serving together as missionaries. Silas was willing to go with Paul and was even arrested and put in jail with him. Ask, how was Silas a good friend to Paul? What can we do to be good friends to others?

104. Barnabas

Barnabas was an influential missionary who served alongside Paul. Together they traveled throughout Judea and Asia Minor. Barnabas was a Levite from Cyprus and cousin of John Mark; his real name was Joseph, but the disciples called him Barnabas after he sold some property and gave the profits to the Church. Acts 11:24 describes him, saying, "For he was a good man, and full of the Holy Ghost and of faith."

Discussion Questions:

1. Barnabas means *son of encouragement* in Hebrew. What does it mean to be an encourager? Share a time when someone encouraged you. What happened?

2. In Acts 9 Barnabas vouches for Saul, who had recently been baptized, when other disciples expressed concern. What do you think motivated Barnabas to vouch for Saul? How might this story apply to us today?

3. Barnabas was very generous in sharing his time and money with the Church. Is this a pattern for how we should serve others or tithe? Why or why not?

For Children:

Purposefully bake too much of a treat. Show your children that there is too much for your family to eat. Ask who you could share the treat with and take time to deliver it. Share the story of Barnabas selling his land and giving the money to the Church. Ask, why do you think Barnabas wanted to share his money with the Church? When was a time someone shared with you?

105. Antioch

Antioch in the Bible is the name of two New Testament cities: Pisidian Antioch and Syrian Antioch. Syrian Antioch was a center Christian worship during Roman times. As an ancient Greek city, located on the Orontes River, it had a significant population of Jewish residents. As a result, many early missionaries, including Barnabas and Paul, visited Antioch to preach. The early converts here were to the first to begin using the term *Christian*.

Discussion Questions:

1. A number of Gentile converts joined the Church in Antioch, causing cultural tension among Church members there. What cultural tensions have you witnessed in your congregation? How can we learn to be more unified in the face of diversity?

2. Antioch was the city to which Paul and Barnabas returned and reported from their mission to Asia Minor. In your opinion, what makes a good return mission report? Whose mission reports do you remember the best? Why?

3. Members in Antioch "[sent] relief unto the brethren which dwelt in Judæa" (Acts 11:29). Have you ever donated to the Church Humanitarian Aid fund or tried to help financially after a disaster? What happened? What prompted this action?

For Children:

Share a news story about a natural disaster or other humanitarian need in the world (be sure to consider what is age appropriate). Share the story of Saints living in Antioch sending relief to the Saints in Judea who were suffering from a drought. Explain that the Church helps to provide relief and assistance to people suffering in this kind of crisis. Ask, why do you think the Lord wants us to help send relief to people suffering from natural disasters? What can we do to assist people who need help and relief today?

106. Paul and Silas in Jail

While serving as missionaries in Macedonia, Paul and Silas were arrested, beaten, and placed in jail with their feet held in stocks. In the night, while Paul and Silas sang and praised God, there was an earthquake that shook the prison doors open and loosed the stocks. The jailer awoke and worried all the prisoners had escaped, but Paul called out saying they were all accounted for. As a result of this experience the jailer was converted and baptized (see Acts 16:22-33).

Discussion Questions:

1. Why do you think Paul and Silas sang and praised God after being beaten and arrested? What comfort does song and prayer bring to you in times of trial?

2. Why do you think Paul and Silas did not try to escape when the earthquake provided the opportunity? What would you have done in this situation? Why?

3. In your opinion, what explains the immediate conversion of the jailer? How might the jailer have been prepared to receive the gospel of Jesus Christ?

For Children:

Find a pair of trick handcuffs and teach the children how to magically escape from them. Explain that in old times, jails often used stocks, which were like handcuffs used on the ankles or prisoners. After, tell the story of Paul and Silas in jail in stocks when the earthquake struck, and they could have escaped but did not. Ask, why do you think Paul and Silas did not try to escape when the earthquake provided the opportunity? Why was the jailer willing to be taught the gospel?

107. Mars Hill

Mars Hill is a hill in Athens, Greece (also known as the Hill of Ares), not far from the Acropolis and a local marketplace. The Areopagus Court, the highest court in Greece for civil, criminal, and religious matters, met on Mars Hill at the time of Roman occupation. During Paul's second missionary journey to Athens, he saw how the people were struggling with idolatry. Paul gave a famous speech on Mars Hill called "TO THE UNKNOWN GOD" (Acts 17:23). In his speech Paul taught that we are all God's children.

Discussion Questions:

1. Paul was likely one of only a few Christians in all of Athens when he visited Mars Hill. If you were him, would you be willing to tell others about Jesus? How would you feel in this situation?

2. When giving his speech on Mars Hill, Paul's audience was filled with politicians, lawyers, and leaders. How did Paul know what to say to them? Would you be nervous speaking in front of such an important group of people?

3. Paul says in his speech, "For we are also his offspring" (Acts 17:28). How do you feel about being a child of God? How does knowing you are a child of God impact your self-concept or your behavior?

For Children:

Sing together the song "I Am a Child of God" (*Hymns* p. 301), then read together Acts 17:28-29. Explain that offspring is another word meaning the child of. Tell the children the Greeks worshiped gods made of gold, silver, and stone; but Heavenly Father is a living being. Ask, why does Paul want the Greeks to know they are children of God? How does knowing you are a child of God make you feel?

108. Paul Is Shipwrecked

After being falsely accused and imprisoned, Paul was taken under military guard on a ship going to Rome. Paul told the Romans on the ship, "Sirs, I perceive that this voyage will be with hurt and much damage" (Acts 27:10); but Paul's warning went unheeded. Storms pushed the ship far off course and much of the cargo was thrown overboard to stay afloat. An angel appeared to Paul, saying no lives would be lost, just the ship. Eventually the ship ran aground near Malta and everyone on board survived.

Discussion Questions:

1. After being shipwrecked the people of Malta treated Paul with "no little kindness" (meaning unusual kindness; Acts 28:2). What needs might the shipwrecked crew and passengers have had? How can we be more like the people of Malta?

2. The Centurion over Paul did not listen to his warning of danger. What warnings have the latter-day apostles given recently in general conference? What dangers might occur if we fail to listen to their warnings?

3. After the ship ran aground some of the soldiers suggested killing the prisoners, but the Centurion was willing to save them. Why do you think the Centurion allowed Paul and the other prisoners to live? What does this say about the Centurion?

For Children:

Use a sheet and a toy boat or shoe box to help tell the story of Paul being shipwrecked. Spread the sheet out and have family members sit along the edge around it. During the part of the story where the ocean is calm, leave the sheet on the floor. When the storm starts, have family members grasp the edge of the sheet and make waves that toss the boat around. After finishing the story, ask, what do you think it was like on the boat during the storm? How was Paul able to stay calm despite the danger?

109. Apollos

Acts 18:24 reveals Apollos was a Jewish man "born at Alexandria." Apollos was converted to Christianity while in Ephesus. He had already believed in John the Baptist's teachings, but Aquila and Priscilla "expounded unto him the way of God more perfectly" (Acts 18:26). Later, Apollos's name is mentioned in association with a conflict among Saints who were aligning with specific missionaries.

Discussion Questions:

1. Apollos was known for being "mighty in the Scriptures" (Acts 18:24). What steps have you taken to improve your knowledge of scripture? What has worked for you personally?

2. Apollos knew "only the baptism of John" (Acts 18:25), but was willing to listen to Aquila and Priscilla. What does this say about Apollos? What do you learn from Apollos's humility?

3. Aquila and Priscilla "expounded unto [Apollos] the way of God more perfectly" (Acts 18:26), just as missionaries today teach by building on common beliefs. What beliefs of other faiths do you see that are similar to Latter-day Saint beliefs? What good practices do you see in other faiths?

For Children:

Have your children trace a hand on a piece of paper. In the center of the palm have them write "5 Characteristics of Apollos." Tell the story of Apollos's conversion by reading Acts 18:24-26. Have the children make note of each of the following on the fingers of the traced hand: born in Alexandria, spoke clearly, mighty in the scriptures, spiritual, and good teacher. After, ask, what kind of man was Apollos? How good of a missionary do you think Apollos was once he was converted? Why?

110. Priscilla and Aquila

Priscilla and Aquila were a married couple from Rome who served in various branches of the early Church and were especially helpful to the apostle Paul. The couple seem to interact as equals, unlike the norms of the time that treated women as property. Together Priscilla and Aquila ran a tentmaking business, occasionally hiring Paul as an employee. Priscilla and Aquila were successful missionaries and were instrumental in teaching Apollos about Jesus Christ.

Discussion Questions:

1. Priscilla and Aquila served effectively as a missionary couple in the early days of the Church. In what ways are senior missionaries today more effective than younger elders and sisters? Why are they so effective?

2. Aquila and Priscilla "expounded unto [Apollos] the way of God more perfectly" (Acts 18:26). What do you think this approach looked like? Why is proving someone wrong a poor strategy in missionary work?

3. Priscilla seems to have had a true partnership with her husband, Aquila. In your opinion, what is a partnership? What is needed to help make partnerships work well?

For Children:

Compete in a three-legged race with your child by using a bandanna to tie your legs together at the ankle. Be careful not to trip and injure one another during the race! After, explain that the race required the partners work together in order to win. Share the story of Priscilla and Aquila running a business together and working as missionaries with each other. Ask, in what ways did Priscilla and Aquila need to work together to succeed? How should we treat those we work with if we want to do well?

111. Claudius Caesar

Claudius Caesar served as Roman emperor from 41 to 54 A.D. Known for having poor health, he was ostracized by his family until he unexpectedly came to the throne after the assassination of Gaius Caesar. Claudius was responsible for the expulsion of Jews from Rome sometime around 51 A.D. He forced them out because they were protesting the teaching of Christianity. It was at this time that Priscilla and Aquila were forced to leave and went to Corinth, where they met Paul.

Discussion Questions:

1. As Christianity was being taught in Rome, the Jews began to cause disturbances, leading Claudius to expel them. What challenges have you experienced as you have tried to do the Lord's work?

2. Claudius Caesar suffered from physical disabilities, including a limp and speech impediment. How can we better include and accommodate those with disabilities around us?

3. Known to be studious with an interest in history and law, Claudius Caesar was well-educated. If you could study any subject, what would you choose? Why? How would you use that knowledge?

For Children:

Have a read-a-thon and let each child choose their favorite books. Read the books aloud to the children, pointing out something learned from each book. Afterward, tell the children about Claudius Caesar, the emperor of Rome during part of the New Testament time. Explain that Claudius Caesar liked to study books, particularly those about history and law. Ask, why do you think reading and studying was important to Claudius Caesar? How do you feel about reading? If you could study any subject, what would you choose? Why?

112. Rome

Although not mentioned in the Old Testament, Rome is a prominent location mentioned in the New Testament because the of rise of the Roman Empire. Rome ruled much of the Mediterranean world during the life of the Savior. Because of a decree by Roman Emperor Caesar Augustus, Mary and Joseph traveled to Bethlehem, fulfilling the prophecy indicating where the Christ Child would be born. Later, Pontius Pilate was the Roman governor who sentenced Jesus to death. Roman rule, which built an extensive system of roads and decreed a common language of the people, was instrumental in helping to spread Christianity.

Discussion Questions:

1. Jesus taught, "Render therefore unto Caesar the things which are Caesar's; and unto God the things that are God's" (Matt. 22:21). What do you think this means? What was Christ trying to help us understand?

2. Ultimately Rome became the center of Catholicism and the location of the Vatican. In your opinion, how has the Catholic Church impacted the growth of Christianity?

3. In 313 A.D., the Roman emperor Constantine issued the Edict of Milan, which granted Christianity—as well as most other religions—legal status. In your opinion, what is the value of religious freedom in a nation? Why should religious freedoms be upheld?

For Children:

Find a variety of coins to show the children. Look at the details on the coins, such as dates, pictures, and sayings. Point out the national identity that's included on the coins. Tell the children about the rule of the Roman Empire, about Jesus being asked about paying tribute to Caesar, and the Lord's famous response using a Roman coin (see Matt. 22:17-22). Explain that Christ taught we should respect laws and pay the government what is needed. Ask, how did the Savior react when He went before Roman leaders or was placed on trial? Why does the Savior want us to obey the law?

113. Epistles

Typically, a letter is a form of communication between persons who are apart from each other. Letters are usually confidential and personal in nature. An epistle, on the other hand, is an artistic literary form, similar to dialog or oration. Despite similarity in medium to a letter, an epistle is intended for an audience, to be read aloud in a public setting. In the New Testament times, when communication with distant branches of the church was challenging, the apostles would send epistles to be read aloud to the members.

Discussion Questions:

1. What letters can you think of today that are read over the pulpit at church? What are your thoughts about these "epistles"? Should they be considered scripture? Why or why not?

2. How do you think the church members in the New Testament times felt about getting an epistle or letter from an apostle? Which latter-day prophet or apostle would you like to receive an epistle from? Why?

3. What do you think would be challenging about writing an epistle to a church congregation? How might it be similar to or different from writing a talk?

For Children:

Teach the children how to write and mail a letter by having them send a card or write a thank you note to a friend or family member. Explain that in Bible times some apostles would write letters to whole church congregations; these letters, called epistles, would be read out loud to the members. Read 1 Corinthians 1:1-2 and point out the similarities to a letter greeting. Ask, how do you think the church members felt about getting a letter from an apostle? Which prophet or apostle would you like to receive an epistle from? Why?

114. Epistle to the Romans

The Epistle to the Romans is the sixth book in the New Testament and is the longest of the epistles included as scripture. It was likely written by the apostle Paul while he was in Corinth, sometime around 55-57 A.D. In the epistle Paul praises the Romans for their faith in Christ and condemns idol worship. Two prominent themes in Romans include hope in salvation through the Atonement and the power of the gospel to change or transform people to be more like the Savior.

Discussion Questions:

1. Romans 5:8 Paul wrote, "But God commendeth his love toward us, in that, while we were yet sinners, Christ died for us." What do you think Paul meant when he wrote that "God commendeth his love toward us"? Share a time when you felt the love of God. What happened?

2. Paul teaches the Romans that "the wages of sin is death" (Romans 6:23). What do you think Paul meant? Why do some people seem to have positive outcomes when they sin?

3. How do we promote Paul's counsel that "we, being many, are one body in Christ," (Romans 12:5)? Why is unity so important in the Church?

For Children:

Children in ancient Rome sometimes played a game called Battledore, which is similar to badminton. To play, use a racket or paddle and hit a pinecone or other round object back and forth to each other, working together to keep the object up in the air. After playing, explain that the Apostle Paul sent an epistle to the Saints living in ancient Rome. In the epistle Paul wrote that "we, being many, are one body in Christ," (Romans 12:5). Ask, why is learning to work together important? What blessings come from being unified?

115. First Epistle to the Corinthians

First Corinthians was written by the Apostle Paul while he was in Ephesus. It was delivered to the Saints in Corinth by Paul's scribe Sosthenes sometime around 55-56 A.D. Paul wrote the epistle after hearing about struggles the Saints in Corinth were experiencing with idol worship, immorality, and other pagan practices. Paul's discourse on gifts of the spirit in 1 Corinthians 12 is comparable to Moroni 7 and D&C 46. His words on charity in 1 Corinthians 13 are arguably some of the most beloved verses in the New Testament.

Discussion Questions:

1. Paul emphasized the importance of "the keeping of the commandments of God" (1 Corinthians 7:19). How has keeping the commandments blessed your life? What commandments do you find easier or harder to follow?

2. Paul taught, "Know ye not that ye are the temple of God, and that the Spirit of God dwelleth in you?" (1 Cor. 3:16). How is the body like a temple? What practices do you follow to take care of your body?

3. Consider the different types of gifts of the spirit mentioned in 1 Corinthians 12. Which gifts do you think you might have? Which gift would you like to have? Why?

For Children:

Make a list of gifts your children would like to receive for a birthday or other holiday. Ask why they want these different gifts. Explain that the Lord also gives us gifts. Ask, what are some of the gifts God has given you? Share some of the gifts listed in 1 Corinthians 12, explaining what they are as needed. Then ask, which of these gifts would you like to receive someday? Why?

116. Second Epistle to the Corinthians

Second Corinthians was written by the Apostle Paul while he was in Macedonia, not long after the epistle of 1 Corinthians. Titus brought word to Paul that the Saints in Corinth were making progress after receiving his counsel, but the people were still struggling with some false teachings. In response to this news, Paul wrote again to the Corinthians to encourage and strengthen them in the gospel. He also asks them to send financial support to the Saints in Jerusalem who were struggling.

Discussion Questions:

1. Paul describes the Savior as "the God of all comfort" (1 Cor. 1:3). How do you find comfort in Christ? What steps do you take to seek out that comfort in your life?

2. How do we "walk by faith, not by sight," as Paul taught in 2 Cor. 5:7? Share a time you had to exercise your faith in the Atonement. What happened?

3. In 2 Cor. 12:2-4 Paul shares a sacred personal experience he had being "caught up to the third heaven." What do you think it would be like having a vision of the celestial kingdom? What would you hope to see or find in the celestial kingdom?

For Children:

Take the children on a nature walk. Look for plants with thorns or prickly parts. Help the children carefully touch a few thorns or spines so they can feel how barbed and dangerous they can be. Share the Apostle Paul's comment, "There was given to me a thorn in the flesh," (2 Cor. 12:7). Explain that Paul had a trial that was causing him pain like a thorn poking him. Ask, what kinds of trials would be like thorns pricking you? What should we do when we have a painful trial?

117. Emperor Nero

Nero was the 5th emperor of Rome, ruling from 54 to 68 A.D. Nero was known to have a charismatic personality, but caused scandals by having family members killed and by marrying another man's wife. Paul was imprisoned in Rome while serving his third missionary journey. Instead of being sent back to Jerusalem for trial, Paul appealed to Emperor Nero for a court hearing. Although he never met with Nero, Paul was able to teach the gospel to some in the royal household. Nero's persecution of Christians likely led to the deaths of Peter and Paul.

Discussion Questions:

1. Emperor Nero was known for persecuting the Christians. Have you ever been persecuted for your religious beliefs? What can we do to help prevent religious persecution today?

2. Paul was never able to get a court hearing before Emperor Nero. How do you think he endured his two years in prison waiting? What can we do to be productive, even when life isn't going the way we want it to?

3. Nero competed in the Olympic 10-horse chariot race and was declared the winner. Who are your favorite Olympians or athletes from history? How is being an Olympic athlete similar to having faith in Christ?

For Children:

Use one of the online tutorials (like the one on ehow.com) to help the children make Roman laurel leaf crowns. While working to make a crown, tell the children about the Emperor Nero and Paul asking for a court hearing for two years. Explain that Nero persecuted Christians and was mean to them. Ask, why do you think Nero refused to give Paul a court hearing? What should we do when people treat us badly because of our faith in Christ?

118. Epistle to the Galatians

The Epistle to the Galatians was written by Paul while in Macedonia around 55-57 A.D. The Kingdom of Galatia, located in the area of modern-day Turkey, had become a province of the Roman Empire. The Saints there were struggling and reverting back to living the Law of Moses. Paul wrote to the Galatians to urge them to rely on the salvation offered through Christ's Atonement and to clarify that the Law of Moses had been fulfilled.

Discussion Questions:

1. Paul testifies that Christ "gave himself for our sins, that he might deliver us from this present evil world, according to the will of God and our Father" (Gal. 1:4). How did Christ give Himself for our sins?

2. We learn from Paul that "if ye be Christ's, then are ye Abraham's seed, and heirs according to the promise" (Gal. 3:29). How can we know if we are Abraham's seed? How is the Gathering of Israel related to this promise?

3. Paul teaches how the spirit feels in Galatians 5:22-23: "love, joy, peace, longsuffering, gentleness, goodness, faith, Meekness, temperance." Which of these do you relate to the most when feeling the influence of the Holy Ghost? Share a time when you felt the spirit strongly. What happened?

For Children:

Create a fruit of the spirit tree. Draw a large tree on a piece of paper, then have the children draw small pictures symbolizing each of the feelings Paul mentioned in Gal. 5:22-23 (e.g., draw a heart for love, a smiley face for joy, a dove for peace, etc.). Cut out the small pictures and have the children glue them on the tree as the fruits. Ask, how do you know when you are feeling the Holy Ghost? What does it feel like to you?

119. Epistle to the Ephesians

While under house arrest in Rome, Paul wrote the Epistle to the Ephesians (about 60 AD). Although Ephesians 1:1 indicates the epistle was written to the Saints in Ephesus, the earliest manuscripts of the epistle do not contain this description. Instead, scholars tend to believe the letter was written to gentile members of the Church (see Eph. 2:11). Elder Bruce R. McConkie said "Ephesians is an epistle for all the world," (*Doctrinal New Testament Commentary*, 3 vols. [1965–73], 2:489). In Ephesians, Paul gives his famous discourse on the purpose of the Church; he discusses the organization of the church including prophets, apostles, evangelists, etc.; and explains the necessity of putting on the armor of God.

Discussion Questions:

1. Considering Elder McConkie's belief that Ephesians is written to the world, what do you think the world could or should learn from this it? Share something you have learned personally from Ephesians.

2. Paul tells us, "Ye are no more strangers and foreigners, but fellowcitizens with the saints, and of the household of God" (Eph. 2:19). Do you think most Church members feel loved and accepted this way? What should we do if we don't feel accepted in the household of God?

3. Why does Paul emphasize the need for "One Lord, one faith, one baptism, One God" (Eph. 4:5-6)? How might this teaching apply to us today?

For Children:

Watch the Schoolhouse Rock video of "The Great American Melting Pot" (available to watch on YouTube). Explain that when a person comes to live in a new country, usually they become a new citizen. Read Ephesians 2:19 and explain that getting baptized and becoming a member of the Church is like becoming a citizen of a new country. Ask, what do you think Paul meant about being a "fellowcitizen"? How can we show love and acceptance to newly baptized Church members?

120. Armor of God

While writing to the Ephesians, the apostle Paul encouraged the Saints to "take unto you the whole armour of God, that ye may be able to withstand in the evil day" (Ephesians 6:13). Paul knew the Saints would be tempted by Satan and persecuted by those around them; they would need protection. The armor consists of six pieces: truth to girt the loins, a breastplate of righteousness, feet shod with the gospel of peace, a shield of faith, helmet of salvation, and a sword of Spirit, meaning the word of God. To wear the armor of God requires followers of Christ to make a daily conscious effort to follow the example of the Savior.

Discussion Questions:

1. What part of the armor of God has blessed you the most in your life (Eph. 6:13-18)? What part of the armor do you find difficult to put on or keep on?

2. In your opinion, is it possible to "put on" only part of the armor at any one time? Why or why not? Why might someone only use part of the armor of God and not all of it?

3. What part of us does the breastplate of righteousness cover? What is the purpose of this piece of armor?

For Children:

Print out one of the many armor of God paper dolls available online and let the children color and cut out the pieces. Read Paul's description of the armor of God in Eph. 6:13-18 and teach the children how each piece of the armor protects. Ask, what part of the armor do you think is the most important? Why? How do we put the armor of God on in real life?

121. Epistle to the Philippians

The Epistle to the Philippians was written by the Apostle Paul, likely with Timothy as his scribe, while Paul was under house arrest in Rome around 60 A.D. Located in Greece, Philippi was the first place where Paul taught the gospel in Europe (Acts 16). Epaphroditus, a member of the Philippi congregation, had been sent to minister to Paul during his house arrest. On the way home to Philippi, Epaphroditus took this epistle with him. In the epistle Paul offers encouragement, counsel, and warnings.

Discussion Questions:

1. Paul declares, "I can do all things through Christ which strengtheneth me" (Philippians 4:13). What is something you have done through the strength of Christ? How does Christ strengthen you?

2. Paul thanks the Philippians for their "fellowship in the gospel" (Philippians 1:5). What experiences have you had fellowshipping new Church members or those who are struggling? What does effective fellowshipping look or feel like?

3. Philippians 4:8 was used by Joseph Smith when he wrote the 13th Article of Faith. Share a time you sought after something "pure," "lovely," "of good report," or of "praise." What sparked your interest? What happened?

For Children:

Write each of the ten words found in Philippians 4:13 on different sticky notes. Have the children try to put the words in the correct order. Look the verse up in the scriptures together if needed to get the order correct. Explain that following Jesus brings us strength; He enables us to serve others, overcome weaknesses, and follow the commandments. Ask, what is something you have done through the strength of Christ? How does Christ strengthen you?

122. Epistle to the Colossians

The Epistle to the Colossians was written by Paul, likely near the same time the epistles to the Philippians and Ephesians were written. The epistle was written after Paul received a visit from Epaphras, one of the members from Colossae. In the letter, Paul emphasizes the role of Jesus Christ as "the head of all principality and power" (Col. 2:10). The Saints in Colossae (modern-day Turkey) were instructed to share this epistle with those in nearby Laodicea (Col. 4:16).

Discussion Questions:

1. Paul sends greetings to some of his "fellowworkers unto the kingdom of God, which have been a comfort unto me" (Col. 4:11). Who would you say were the "fellowworkers" that you enjoyed serving with the most in your callings? How did serving together help bring you comfort or friendship?

2. Colossians 2:2 states, "Set your affection on things above, not on things on the earth." What earthly things do you see people putting their affection on? How can we overcome having a tendency toward materialism?

3. Paul encourages the Colossae Saints to put "filthy communication out of your mouth" (Col. 3:8). Why is cursing considered a bad habit? What strategies can we use to stop using profanity?

For Children:

Hold a finger-painting session as a family. After, point out how "filthy" hands get when finger painting. Explain that filthy means dirty or unclean. Read Col. 3:8 and discuss what "filthy communication" might mean. Ask, why is cursing filthy? What strategies can we use to stop using profanity?

123. Epistles to the Thessalonians

Paul wrote two epistles to the Saints in Thessalonica, now the second largest city in Greece. The first epistle is considered the earliest of all the Pauline epistles included in the New Testament. Both Thessalonian epistles were written during Paul's second missionary journey in about 50 A.D., and both were likely written from Corinth. Paul discusses themes related to the Second Coming of Christ and appeals to the Saints to stand firm in the gospel.

Discussion Questions:

1. Paul says in both epistles to the Thessalonians that he makes mention of them in his prayers. Who do you mention frequently in your prayers? How can praying for others impact your relationship with them? Share a personal experience you had praying with others.

2. 1 Thessalonians 4:16 says, "For the Lord himself shall descend from heaven with a shout, with the voice of the archangel." What do you think an archangel sounds like? Would you like to witness this? Why or why not?

3. Paul teaches in 2 Thessalonians 2:3, "Let no man deceive you by any means: for that day shall not come, except there come a falling away first." What falling away took place after Paul's death? Why do you think a falling away had to happen?

For Children:

Find a way to engage your children in a service project or other wholesome activity. After, ask the children if they enjoyed it or if they got tired during the project. Share 2 Thessalonians 3:13, where Paul tells the Saints to "be not weary in well doing." Explain that to be weary means getting tired or worn out. Ask, why is it sometimes tiring to give service? What can we do to make sure we don't get weary?

124. Timothy

Timothy was an early Christian, born to a Greek Father and a Jewish mother, who was a follower of Christ. In his youth, Timothy's mother and grandmother, Eunice and Lois, nurtured his love for the scriptures. Paul mentored Timothy and circumcised him so those of Jewish heritage would be more accepting of him. Timothy became a trusted assistant and missionary companion to Paul, suffering great persecution and imprisonment. In later years Timothy was called as the first bishop in Ephesus.

Discussion Questions:

1. Timothy's mother and grandmother had great faith in Christ. Who were some the first members of your friends or family to join the Church? What happened? How has their faith influenced you?

2. Timothy is mentored by Paul. Why would Paul take the time and energy to mentor Timothy? How can we mentor others in the gospel?

3. Paul counsels Timothy to "be thou an example of the believers, in word, in conversation, in charity, in spirit, in faith, in purity" (1 Tim. 4:12). How can we be an example to others in the words we choose to use in conversation? How can we be an example of charity?

For Children:

Tell your children about the first person in your family who joined the Church. If possible, show pictures and artifacts related to the story. After, tell the children about Timothy, whose mother and grandmother were early Christian converts and raised him to have a love of the scriptures. Explain that later Timothy was a mission companion to Paul and a bishop in Ephesus. Ask, how do you think the faith of Timothy's mother and grandmother influenced him? How might the faith of our ancestors influence us?

125. Epistles to Timothy

There are two epistles written by Paul to Timothy in the New Testament. These epistles, sometimes called pastoral epistles, focus more on administrative matters to help Timothy in his role as a leader in the church. These epistles were likely not written to be read to the members of Timothy's congregation. Paul wrote the epistles in about 65 A.D. after serving two years of house arrest in Rome. Paul appears to have considered Timothy to be like a son; Paul's effort to mentor Timothy as a leader in the Church shows his faith and trust in the younger man.

Discussion Questions:

1. Paul mentions that Timothy's mother and grandmother were very influential in helping to teach him the scriptures. Who in your life reached out and helped you to better understand the gospel? What did they do?

2. Paul prophesies that in the latter days some will be led away from the gospel by those "commanding to abstain from meats" (1 Tim. 4:3). Do you see this happening in the world today? Why do some say not to eat meat? How does this align with the Word of Wisdom?

3. Paul tells Timothy that "in the last days perilous times shall come" (2 Tim. 3:1). What is perilous about the times we live in? How do you protect yourself from the perils of our day?

For Children:

Share with your children something you learned from your mother and from your grandmother. If possible, show pictures of these women and explain how you learned from them. Tell the children that Timothy, a church leader in the New Testament, was taught to love the scriptures by his grandmother, Lois, and mother Eunice. Ask, why do you think Timothy's mother and grandmother wanted him to learn about the scriptures? What is something you would like to learn from your mother or grandmother?

126. Titus

Titus was a faithful servant of the Lord and a dedicated assistant to Paul. In fact, Paul called him "my partner and fellowhelper" (2 Cor. 8:23). As a Gentile, Titus converted to Christianity after being taught by Paul. He was asked to strengthen the Church in Corinth and later served alongside Paul as a missionary. Apparently, Titus had strong administrative abilities; he was told to "set in order the things that are wanting" in Crete (Titus 1:5).

Discussion Questions:

1. Titus was the first bishop of the church of the Cretans. Who is a bishop who made a difference in your life? What did you learn from him?

2. Paul told Titus to confront false doctrine being taught and to train Church members in the truth. What do you do if you hear someone teach something incorrect at Church? What is the best way to handle such a situation?

3. Church leaders should be blameless or above reproach (Titus 1:6-7). What's the difference between blameless and sinless? How should leaders behave to be considered above reproach?

For Children:

Coach your children in a favorite family sport, such as soccer, baseball, volleyball, etc. Spend some time practicing and giving good coaching advice. Explain that a coach's job is to help players learn how to do things and to perform well in a game. At church, one of the coaches we have is the bishop. Share the story of Titus being asked to serve as the bishop in Crete and being given advice by Paul on how to serve the people. Ask, what makes a good bishop? What bishop(s) have made a difference in your life? What have you learned from your bishop(s)?

127. Epistle to Titus

In approximately 65 A.D. the Apostle Paul wrote the epistle to Titus, at about the same time he wrote the epistles to Timothy. Titus was a Greek who had been taught and converted to the gospel by Paul. At the time of the writing of the epistle, Titus is serving as a leader in the Church at Crete; Paul's writing was to strengthen and support Titus in his efforts there, as well as offer administrative advice. Most likely writing from Macedonia, Paul sent the epistle with Zenas and Apollos, who were on a journey that took them through Crete.

Discussion Questions:

1. Paul calls Titus "mine own son after the common faith" (Titus 1:4). How do those we teach the gospel become like sons or daughters? What similarities to real sons or daughters do you see in this?

2. Paul encourages Titus to be "looking for that blessed hope" (Titus 2:13). Why does Paul give this advice? How do you look for hope in your life?

3. Why does Paul give the counsel to avoid "contentions, and strivings about the law" (Titus 3:9)? How well do you feel those around you follow this counsel today? What problems do contentions and strivings lead to?

For Children:

Play a game of Punch Bug. Identify a color or type of vehicle family members should look for while driving. The first person to see a vehicle that fits the description calls out, "Punch bug!" and gets a point. Keep score during the duration of the game. Each correct identification of a vehicle earns one point, but a mistake causes the loss of a point. After the game, ask the children if they saw more of that type of car than they likely would have if they had not been playing the game or looking for it. Explain that the same thing happens when we "[look] for that blessed hope" (Titus 2:13) in life. Ask, how can we look for blessings or things to be hopeful about in life? What is a blessing you have received lately?

128. Philemon

Philemon was a convert to the Church, taught by Paul in his missionary travels to Asia minor. Although there is no information about his conversion story, Paul's epistle to Philemon reveals he was a wealthy slave owner who hosted a congregation of the Church in his home in Colossae. One of Philemon's slaves, Onesimus, ran away and was converted to Christianity. The purpose of Paul's epistle to Philemon was to ask him to forgive Onesimus and receive him back as a brother in the gospel.

Discussion Questions:

1. Paul refers to himself as "a prisoner of Jesus Christ" (Philemon 1:9). What do you think Paul means by this phrase? In what way are we prisoners of Christ?

2. Philemon is being asked to forgive Onesimus. What does forgiveness look or feel like to you? Share a time you either forgave or sought forgiveness from another.

3. Paul sends Onesimus back to Philemon. Was it right for Onesimus to be sent back into slavery? What are the dangers of holding different cultures or periods of history up to modern-day standards?

For Children:

Teach the children the song and actions to Hokey Pokey. After singing it together, explain that turning yourself around is a lot like forgiveness. Share the story of Paul asking Philemon to forgive Onesimus. Ask, what response do you think Philemon had to Paul's epistle? Did he turn himself around and forgive? How can we learn to forgive others?

129. Epistle to Philemon

The Epistle to Philemon was written by Paul as a private letter while he was under house arrest in Rome around 60 A.D. As a letter written to an individual, it does not focus as much on Church doctrine as other epistles in the New Testament. Philemon was a wealthy Greek convert to the Church and a friend of Paul's. Paul's epistle to Philemon was to ask him to forgive his runaway slave, Onesimus, as a brother in the gospel.

Discussion Questions:

1. Paul writes about Onesimus, "[He] in time past was to thee unprofitable, but now profitable to thee and to me" (Philemon 1:11). Why was Onesimus now so much more useful than before? In what ways can new converts to the Church be helpful to congregations?

2. In your opinion, does Onesimus deserve forgiveness? How do you decide who deserves forgiveness? What counsel do the scriptures provide?

3. Paul's letter to Philemon is, in essence, an exercise in mediation. What can we learn about mediation and conflict resolution from the way Paul handles the situation? In your opinion, what is the best way to handle conflict? Share a tip that has worked well for you.

For Children:

Place a backpack on your child for an object lesson about forgiveness. Share several brief scenarios where forgiveness is needed, such as, "Your friend Tom took your favorite toy," or, "Marie did not invite you to her birthday party." After each scenario ask your child if they are willing to forgive. When the answer is no, place a weighty book in the backpack. When removing the books, have your child repeat, "I forgive you," to reinforce the lesson. Share the story of Paul asking Philemon to forgive Onesimus. Ask, does Onesimus deserve forgiveness? What do you think Philemon should do?

130. Epistle to the Hebrews

The Prophet Joseph Smith attributed Hebrews to the Apostle Paul; however, there is no information about exactly where or when the letter was written. From the letter itself it is clear the writer must have had authority in the apostolic church and was an intellectual Hebrew Christian well versed in the scriptures. In the epistle, the author tries to convince the Jewish converts to Christianity not to return to their former faith practices. The epistle reads like a sermon, teaching that the Law of Moses was fulfilled in Christ, the great High Priest of the Melchizedek priesthood. the author urges the Hebrew Saints to "go on unto perfection" by following the Savior (Hebrews 6:1).

Discussion Questions:

1. The author of Hebrews teaches, "Now faith is the substance of things hoped for, the evidence of things not seen" (Hebrews 11:1). What is something you believe in but can't see? How did you come to that belief?

2. According to the author of Hebrews, "The word of God is quick, and powerful, and sharper than any twoedged sword, piercing even to the dividing asunder of soul and spirit" (Hebrews 4:12). Share a time the word of God pierced your soul. What happened?

3. The author tells the Hebrews that Christ is the captain of their salvation (Heb. 2:10). What role does a captain

play to a ship or plane? How is this similar to how Christ helps in our salvation?

For Children:

Make an invisible message to teach the children about faith being evidence of things not seen. Mix some lemon juice and a few drops of water in a bowl. Use a cotton swab to write a message on a blank piece of paper. Let it dry completely. Share Hebrews 11:1 with the children and explain that faith is a belief in something you can't see. Heat the paper by holding it close to a light bulb to reveal the secret message. Ask, what is something you believe in but have not seen? How can we increase our faith in Jesus?

131. James the Just

According to Galatians 1:19, James was a half-sibling of Jesus, and a full sibling to Jude. Christian tradition has it that James was converted after the death and resurrection of his Brother; he saw the resurrected Savior and witnessed of that knowledge (1 Cor. 15:5-8). Eventually James became an apostle and was made the first bishop of the Church in Jerusalem. This James is likely the author of the eponymous book in the New Testament; his words influenced the boy Joseph to pray and ask God for wisdom in the latter-days (James 1:5). James was called "the Just" because of his strict adherence to the commandments, which involved taking Nazarite vows.

Discussion Questions:

1. Why do you think it took so long for James to recognize that his Brother was the long-awaited Messiah? How would you feel if your sibling was similarly famous or accomplished?

2. In James 1:1, James introduces himself as "a servant of God" instead of saying he is a sibling of Jesus Christ. Why do you think James made this choice? What does it say about his character?

3. Why do you think Jesus left his mother, Mary, in the care of John when James (and at least three other brothers; see Matt. 13:55-56) could likely have taken on the responsibility?

For Children:

Play a game of matching brothers. Have one person give the name of a famous character, then let the children try to name the brother. (Child-friendly examples might include Dash and Jack-Jack; Huey, Dewey and Louie; Lucien and Wayne Cramp; Phineas and Ferb; Mufasa and Scar; and Alvin, Simon, and Theodore). After, tell the children that two brothers in the New Testament were Jesus and James. Explain that James did not gain a testimony of the gospel until after Jesus was resurrected. Ask, what do you think it would have been like to be a brother or sister to Jesus?

132. Epistle of James

The General Epistle of James was written by James, one of the half-brothers of Jesus Christ. James accepted the gospel after Jesus appeared to him as a resurrected being (see 1 Corinthians 15:7). In a proverb-like style of writing, James explains basic principles of living the gospel. Some of the major themes addressed in the epistle include wisdom, patient perseverance during trials, and condemnation of sin. The opening verse of the epistle indicates James wrote to all the house of Israel. Some historians date the Epistle of James as being written prior to 50 A.D., making this letter is the earliest of all the New Testament writings — with the possible exception of Galatians.

Discussion Questions:

1. James 1:5 is the well-known verse that led 14-year-old Joseph Smith to pray to ask God for wisdom. What is wisdom? How is it different from or similar to knowledge?

2. James teaches, "Faith without works is dead" (James 2:26). What does this verse mean to you? Is faith without works of any use? Why or why not?

3. James 3:6 states, "The tongue is a fire, a world of iniquity." Share a time you caused yourself trouble by saying the wrong thing? What happened? Why is learning to watch what we say so challenging?

For Children:

Watch the video "Draw Near Unto Me | Animated Scripture Lesson for Kids" (found on YouTube; 4:55 min. in length). After, ask, how can we draw nearer to Jesus? When do you feel closest to Jesus?

133. Epistles of Peter

Peter, originally known as Simon, the fisherman, is the author of two epistles published in the New Testament. Peter was called as the chief apostle, or prophet, by the Savior and was given the keys of the priesthood to lead the Church. The epistles were likely written while Peter was in Rome (Peter says from "Babylon" in 1 Peter 5:13), sometime between 60-64 A.D. His intended audience was members of the Church living in Roman provinces in Asia-minor.

Discussion Questions:

1. What does it mean that we are chosen according to God's foreknowledge (1 Peter 1:2)? How do you feel about foreknowledge? Is it the same as predestination? Why or why not?

2. Peter tells the Saints, "But ye are a chosen generation, a royal priesthood, an holy nation, a peculiar people" (1 Peter 2:9). In what ways does the world consider Church members peculiar today? How do you feel about being thought of as peculiar or weird?

3. Peter writes about how Christ "went and preached unto the spirits in prison" (1 Peter 3:19). What do you envision Christ's visit to spirit prison looked like? What did He preach to them there?

For Children:

Play a few games of hangman with your children using the words *chosen, royal, holy*, and *peculiar*. Explain the meanings of each of these words as needed. Share 1 Peter 2:9 and point out the use of these words to describe Church members. Ask, who considers Church members chosen, royal, and holy? Who considers Church members peculiar? How are members of the Church different from other people in the world?

134. Epistles of John

The three Epistles of John, or the Johannine Epistles, are three letters traditionally attributed to the apostle John (the Beloved, same author as the Book of Revelation). It is unclear who the letters are written to, each appearing to be addressed to different parties, but they were likely written near the end of the first century A.D. The primary themes of these epistles include love of God and Jesus Christ as the Savior. Apostasy, false leaders, and deceivers are also mentioned in each of the epistles.

Discussion Questions:

1. In 1 John the author shares his eyewitness account of Jesus being sent by God to be the Savior of the world. What do you think it would be like to be an eyewitness of the Savior's life? What benefits and challenges would that role present?

2. In 2 John 1:6 we learn, "And this is love, that we walk after his commandments." How is keeping the commandments a form of love? What commandments do you find hard to keep, but you do so out of love?

3. John knew there would be an apostasy before the Second Coming of Christ, yet he warns the Saints about falling away. How would you feel if you were in John's situation? How might John have remained hopeful in the face of the Great Apostasy?

For Children:

Cut out hearts and "heart attack" a neighbor or friend's front door to let them know they are loved. Share the scripture, "We love him, because he first loved us" (1 John 4:19). Explain that God loves each of His children dearly and wants us to return to live with Him again. Ask, how do we know God loves us? How do you feel God's love for you?

135. Jude (Brother of James)

Jude was the brother of James the Just; both Jude and James were half-brothers of the Lord. Although no further details are given in scripture about Jude, he seems to be held in high esteem and may have been a leader in the early Church. Jude is the likely author of the eponymous New Testament book. In the epistle Jude encourages the Saints to "earnestly contend for the faith" (Jude 1:3), especially when false doctrine was taught in the Church. Jude also mentions the concept of pre-existence in Jude 1:6.

Discussion Questions:

1. Jude wrote about "angels which kept not their first estate" (Jude 1:6). Why do you think some angels failed to pass the tests they faced in the pre-existence? What difficulties were there?

2. Jude advises us to, "Keep yourselves in the love of God" (Jude 1:21). What do you think he means by this? How do we keep ourselves in God's love?

3. One of the ideas of Jude's epistle is that we can strengthen others who are weak in the faith. What might you do to help a friend or family member who is struggling with their faith?

For Children:

Ask the children to each draw a picture of what God's love looks like to them. Have each child share their picture with the family and explain their thoughts. Read Jude 1:21 and explain that Jude taught that we need to keep ourselves in the love of God. Ask, how can we follow Jude's advice and stay in God's love?

136. Epistle of Jude

The Epistle of Jude is one of the shortest books in the New Testament and the last of the epistles. Written by Jude, the half-brother of Jesus Christ and brother of James the Just, the epistle infers Jude was a leader in the Church in Jerusalem. The letter is addressed very generally in the first verse of the book and could apply to Jewish Christians, Gentile Christians, or both. The beginning of the Great Apostasy had begun by the time this letter was written (sometime between 40-80 A.D.); a number of the apostles had already been martyred on behalf of their faith.

Discussion Questions:

1. Jude writes that "there are certain men crept in unawares" who are denying Jesus Christ (Jude 1:4). How do incorrect beliefs creep into the Church? What counsel have latter-day prophets and apostles given to help protect members from false doctrines?

2. The Epistle of Jude describes Satan's followers as "the angels which kept not their first estate" (Jude 1:6). What was the first estate? What things did Satan's followers give up when they chose not to come to earth? Which of these things do you think would be the hardest to give up?

3. Jude records a prophecy by Enoch about the Second Coming: "The Lord cometh with ten thousands of his saints, To execute judgment upon all" (Jude 1:15-16).

What do you envision this will look like? Where might it take place? Would you want to be there? Why or why not?

For Children:

Visit the library and pick out books about compassion, helping others, or kindness. After reading some of the books, discuss what it means to be compassionate toward others. Read Jude 1:22, "And of some have compassion, making a difference." Ask, how can showing compassion make a difference in other people's lives? How does it make a difference in your life?

137. John the Beloved

John the Beloved is the brother of James; both brothers were sons of Zebedee and worked as fishermen on the Sea of Galilee prior to following Jesus. John is the author of five of the books in the New Testament, including St. John, the three Epistles of John, and the Book of Revelation. Peter, James, and John served together as leaders over the Church after Christ's resurrection. After Peter's death (in about A.D. 67) John would have been the senior and presiding apostle. For a time, John was exiled on the isle of Patmos, where he received the Book of Revelation. No record exists of John's death.

Discussion Questions:

1. John refers to himself as "the disciple whom Jesus loved" (John 13:23). What does this self-description reveal to you about John's personality? What might it say about his relationship with Christ?

2. John is the only one of the Twelve recorded as being present during the Crucifixion. Why do you think he stayed?

3. James and John both came from a successful family of fishermen. What do you think it was like for them to leave their profession behind to follow Jesus? Would you be willing to leave your profession behind to follow Christ?

For Children:

Play the card game Go Fish together as a family (official rules can be found online at bicyclecards.com/how-to-play/go-fish). After, explain that some of Jesus's disciples, including John, were fishermen before they followed Him. Ask, what do you think it was like for them to leave their profession behind to follow Jesus? Was it easy or hard for them?

138. Aegean Island of Patmos

Patmos is a small Greek island in the Aegean Sea and the site of Roman penal colony. In New Testament times, the island was a destination for criminals and political prisoners who had been banished. Patmos is only mentioned one time in the New Testament. The apostle John indicated that while exiled on the Isle of Patmos he worked on writing the Book of Revelations. In Revelations 1:9 John writes he "was in the isle that is called Patmos, for the word of God, and for the testimony of Jesus Christ."

Discussion Questions:

1. Patmos is only about 13 square miles. How might John have felt being exiled to such a small island? What would you do if you were stuck on a similar sized island?

2. While on Patmos John received a vision of the Savior. How might John's location or surroundings have contributed to his preparation to receive this vision? How do your surroundings influence your ability to feel the spirit?

3. Tradition has it that John's vision was received in a grotto, or cave, halfway up on a mountain on Patmos. Why would this be a good location for John to receive his vision? Where in nature do you like to go to feel closer to God?

For Children:

Play a game of hide and seek, but add a twist: once the seeker finds someone hiding, they are taken to "jail" (a designated spot where they wait until all of the other players are found). After several rounds of the game, share the story of the apostle John being exiled to the Isle of Patmos and writing the Book of Revelation after seeing a vision. Ask, why would this be a good location for John to receive his vision? Where in nature do you like to go to feel closer to God?

139. Book of Revelation

The last book of the New Testament is the Book of Revelation, written by John the Beloved (son of Zebedee) while he was banished to the Isle of Patmos. Also known as the Apocalypse, the book reveals important information about the Second Coming of the Lord and the Millennium. Like Isaiah, Revelation uses vivid imagery that is often difficult for modern-day readers to understand. John originally wrote the book for the seven branches of the Church in Asia-minor, urging them to continue on in their faith despite persecution. One distinctive feature of the Book of Revelation is the frequency of the number seven, which is mentioned 52 times.

Discussion Questions:

1. In 1 Nephi 14:24–29 we learn that although Nephi saw a similar vision, he was told that the Lord commanded John to write about the Second Coming. Why do you think John was assigned to write about it instead of Nephi? Why are some callings or assignments designated for specific people?

2. John wrote that those who will receive God's protection in the last days will have the seal of God in their foreheads. What do you think this seal represents? How do we get the seal on our foreheads?

3. In Revelation 12 John writes about the pre-existence: "And there was war in heaven: Michael and his angels

fought against the dragon." What do you think the war in heaven was like? How was the war fought?

For Children:

Teach the children how to seal an envelope, either by licking the seal or by using candle wax to hold the flap. Explain that the seal helps the person receiving the letter know if the envelope was opened or not. Share with the children the seven seals in the Book of Revelation that are signs of the Second Coming. When opened a judgment on the earth is released (Rev. 6). Ask, why do you think the judgments are sealed up before being opened? Should we be afraid when the seals are opened? Why or why not?

140. Apocalypse

By definition, an apocalypse is a revelation of great divine importance. In Christianity, the Apocalypse is usually a reference to revelation about the end of the world or the Second Coming of Christ. Typically, widespread destruction, war (Armageddon), and natural disasters are associated with the apocalypse. Although the Savior Himself prophesied about the Second Coming in the Olivet Discourse (Matt. 24-25), the Apostle John's Book of Revelation is sometimes called the Apocalypse.

Discussion Questions:

1. One synonym for the Apocalypse is the Great Reveal. What do you think will be revealed in the Great Reveal? How can a person prepare for a revelation of that proportion?

2. Russell M. Nelson has stated that things are moving forward at an accelerated pace toward the Second Coming. What signs of this acceleration have you noticed? What more do you expect to see soon?

3. If you knew the apocalypse would take place in the next few weeks, what preparations would you undertake? Explain.

For Children:

Tell the children you are going to teach them how to make a coin disappear (there are several instruction videos on YouTube if needed). Show the trick a few times, then reveal how it's done. Let the children try doing the trick themselves. Explain that showing how something is done can be called a reveal. In the New Testament a great divine reveal is called an apocalypse. The Apocalypse refers to the end of the earth when Jesus comes again. Ask, is the Apocalypse something to be afraid of, or something to look forward to? Do you wish it would come sooner or later? Explain.

141. Herod the Great

Herod the Great, or Herod I, was the appointed Roman ruler (king) over Judea at the time of Jesus Christ's birth. He is particularly well-known for having rebuilt the temple in Jerusalem. Herod is mentioned in the Gospel of Matthew when the wise men from the east arrive in search of the Christ Child. Herod, after consulting with the priests and scribes, supposedly ordered all male children aged two and under be killed; however, no other historical records corroborate the massacre.

Discussion Questions:

1. Why did Herod run to the chief priests and scribes for answers when the wise men did not return? When you are in need of answers, where do you turn? What has been effective for you?

2. Herod "flew into a rage" (Matt. 2:16) when the wise men did not return to report to him. What does Herod's response say about his view of the Messiah? What about the Messiah made Herod angry?

3. Herod's kingdom highlighted military power, manipulation, greed, and fear of Roman and foreign invasion. What impact did this wickedness likely have on the Jews?

For Children:

Use figurines from a nativity set to tell the story of the wise men stopping to visit Herod the Great while in search of the Christ Child. Explain that when the wise men did not return to report to Herod, that Herod got angry and asked the priests and scribes what the scriptures said about the Messiah. Ask, why do you think King Herod got angry at the wise men? What do you think Herod thought about the baby Jesus?

142. Bethlehem

Bethlehem is a small city located about six miles (10 km) south of Jerusalem and is well-known for growing almonds and olives for olive oil. In Hebrew Bethlehem means "house of bread" (Guide to the Scriptures, "Bethlehem"). Although featured in the Old Testament, Bethlehem plays a prominent role in the New Testament as the birthplace of the Savior. The prophet Micah foretold that Jesus Christ would be born in Bethlehem (Micah 5:2).

Discussion Questions:

1. Would you ever want to visit Bethlehem? Why or why not? What do you think might be interesting to see or do there?

2. Bethlehem was Joseph and Mary's ancestral home. Do you think they were familiar with it and felt welcome there? What kind of family support might they have received while they were in Bethlehem?

3. In what ways did Jesus's Bethlehem ancestors (i.e., Ruth and Boaz, King David, Jesse) influence His life? What lessons can we learn from them?

For Children:

Sing the song "O Little Town of Bethlehem" (*Hymns* 208) and try to help the children learn some of the lyrics. Explain that before Christ was born in Bethlehem, some of His ancestors lived there too. Share a few Old Testament stories about some of these ancestors (i.e., Jacob and Rachel, Ruth and Boaz, Samuel anointing David as King). Ask, in what ways did Jesus's Bethlehem ancestors influence His life? What lessons can we learn from them?

143. Shepherds

Near Bethlehem, there were shepherds tending flocks of sheep. Elder Bruce R. McConkie wrote that these shepherds "watched over, cared for with love and devotion—[sheep that] were destined for sacrifice on the great altar in the Lord's House" (*The Mortal Messiah,* 1:347). On the night of the Savior's birth, choirs of angels appeared to the shepherds in annunciation of the birth of the Lord. After the angels left, the shepherds "came with haste, and found Mary, and Joseph, and the babe lying in a manger" (Luke 2:16).

Discussion Questions:

1. The shepherds immediately went in search of the Christ child after being visited by angels. What can we learn from the example of their behavior?

2. Luke 2:9 says, "The angel of the Lord came upon them." Do you think this might be Gabriel, the same angel who appeared to Mary? Why or why not?

3. Several Christmas songs tell the story of the angels appearing to the shepherds. Which of these songs is your favorite? Why?

For Children:

Hold a family sing-along. At the end of the sing-along, sing one of the Christmas songs that mentions the story of the angels appearing to the shepherds. Review the story after singing. Ask, why do you think God sent a choir to sing after the angel announced Jesus's birth? What kind of songs do you think they sang? Would you like to be a shepherd? Why or why not?

144. Wise Men

As a child, Jesus was visited by Wise Men, or magi, from the east who came in search of Him. "The Wise Men were essentially witnesses of the Savior's birth" (Kenney, Wendy, "We Three Kings." *Ensign*, Dec. 2009, p. 12.). That kings would come to visit the Savior was prophesied of in the Old Testament. In the search for Jesus, the Wise Men sought help from King Herod, who asked them to return and report after they had found the Christ child; however, the Wise Men were warned in a dream not to do so. Matthew 2:11 says the Wise Men brought gifts of gold, frankincense, and myrrh, symbolizing the Savior's kingship, divinity, and eventual death.

Discussion Questions:

1. The Wise Men watched for signs of the Christ child's birth and came when they saw the new star. What signs of the Second Coming are you watching for? How do you plan to act on these signs?

2. If you had a chance to give the Christ child a gift, what would you give to Him? Why?

3. Why do you think these men are described as "wise" (Matt. 2:1)? How can we follow their example and gain more wisdom in our lives?

For Children:

Make paper crowns using construction paper, crayons, and glitter. While working on the crowns, remind the children of the "three" kings in the nativity story. Explain that they came from the east, following the star, in search of the Christ child to bring him gifts. Ask, if you had a chance to give the Christ child a gift, what would you give to Him? Why?

145. Simeon

Simeon was a man in Jerusalem who lived at the time Jesus was born. Luke describes Simeon as being "just and devout," a man waiting "for the consolation of Israel" (Luke 2:25). Joseph and Mary, in obedience to the Law, took baby Jesus to be presented at the temple in Jerusalem. Simeon was prompted by the spirit to go to the temple, as well, where he saw the Christ Child. On taking the baby in his arms Simeon said, "Lord, now lettest thou thy servant depart in peace, according to thy word: For mine eyes have seen thy salvation" (Luke 2:29-30).

Discussion Questions:

1. Simeon had personal revelation that he would not die until he had seen the Savior. How do you think it might have felt for Simeon to wait for this to occur? Would it be harder for him before seeing the Savior, or after?

2. Why do you think Simeon was willing to wait many years to see the Savior? How might he have handled times when he felt impatient or discouraged?

3. Simeon describes the Lord as "A light to lighten the Gentiles" (Luke 2:31). How has the Savior been a light in your life? How can we share the light of Christ with others?

For Children:

Re-enact the marshmallow test with your children. Place a marshmallow or other favorite treat on a plate in front of them. Explain that they can eat it now, or if they wait 15 minutes, they can also have a second marshmallow. Leave them alone in the room to see what choice they make. After returning to the room, ask them about waiting to eat it. Was it easy or hard? Share the story of Simeon waiting to meet the Christ Child. Ask, why do you think Simeon was willing to wait many years to see the Savior? How might he have handled times when he felt impatient or discouraged?

146. Anna the Prophetess

Anna was a prophetess and widow "of great age" (Luke 2:36) who served in the temple. When Mary and Joseph visited the temple with baby Jesus, Anna recognized the child as the Messiah when the Holy Ghost moved upon her. Anna was likely over 100 years old and had been widowed for over 80 years. Her diligence in fasting and prayer in the temple resulted in the blessing of being a witness to the Savior.

Discussion Questions:

1. Anna waited many years to see the Christ Child. Share an experience you've had when you had to wait for a long time for something to take place. What can we learn about endurance and faith from Anna's experience?

2. Anna spent many years serving in the temple. How might her time in the temple have influenced her ability to recognize the Savior? How might it have helped her as she waited for the blessing to take place?

3. What are the similarities and differences in the roles of prophet and prophetess? How does Anna fulfill her role as a prophetess?

For Children:

Ask the children what age a person is when they become "old." Discuss some of the difficulties people have when they get older. Share the story of Anna in Luke 2:36-38. Explain that Anna was likely over 100 years old when she finally saw the Christ Child. Ask, why do you think the Lord let her wait for so many years? What can we learn from Anna's example?

147. War in Heaven

The Apostle John is one of the few Biblical authors to mention the pre-existence. In Revelation, John wrote about the War in Heaven, explaining "Michael and his angels fought against the dragon; and the dragon [Lucifer] fought and his angels, And prevailed not" (Rev. 12:7-8). Additional revelation found in the Doctrine and Covenants confirms that Satan wanted to usurp the power and glory of the Father and rebelled when his plan was rejected, and Jesus was chosen as the Savior. Revelation 12:4 indicates "a third part of the hosts of heaven" followed Lucifer in his rebellion.

Discussion Questions:

1. What do you think the War in Heaven was like? What do you imagine your role in the War in Heaven to have been?

2. Lucifer and his followers still continue to war against those here on earth. What do you think are the greatest weapons they are using against people? How can we fight back?

3. Why is it important to understand what happened in the pre-existence? How can this knowledge benefit us? How has is helped you personally?

For Children:

Listen to the Primary song (or watch a sing-along video) "I Lived in Heaven" (*CS* p. 4). Read the lyrics and review the story of the War in Heaven. Ask, what do you think the War in Heaven was like? Why was Satan mad enough to fight against Heavenly Father, Jesus Christ, Michael, and the angels?

148. Babylon

Babylon was a famous city of antiquity, the capital of Babylonia. It survived for over a thousand years and was important in two separate dynasties. Located on the banks of the Euphrates River (south of modern-day Baghdad, Iraq), Babylon was in a prime spot for commercial trade routes. During the Neo-Babylonian Empire (about 700 - 550 B.C.), Babylon became known for its military might and great wealth. The Apostle John referred to Babylon in the Book of Revelation as a metaphor for pride, greed, and sin.

Discussion Questions:

1. Babylon is used in the scriptures to symbolize pride, greed, and sin. What other cities do you think could be used as a similar metaphor? Why? What characteristics do these cities have in common?

2. The wealth in Babylon was a key reason for its sinful state. Is it bad to be wealthy? Why or why not? How can a person be wealthy and righteous?

3. Is it possible to "live in" or trade with Babylon and not be affected? In what ways do we struggle between our culture and making the Savior the priority?

For Children:

Print out one of the Bible worksheet game pages on sundayschoolzone.com. Explain that after King Nebuchadnezzar II destroyed Jerusalem, he took the Jews to Babylon, where they lived in exile for about 70 years. Babylon was a city of great wealth, parks, and culture. Babylon is used in the scriptures to symbolize pride, greed, and sin. Ask, is it possible to "live in" or trade with Babylon and not be affected? How can we follow Christ when we live in "Babylon"?

149. Angel in the Midst of Heaven

John wrote in Revelation 14:6, "I saw another angel fly in the midst of heaven, having the everlasting gospel to preach unto them that dwell on the earth." This prophecy was fulfilled when the angel Moroni appeared to Joseph Smith and brought him the gold plates to translate. Those Saints left in Nauvoo in 1846 to finish the temple were in part tasked with finishing a gilded flying angel to place on the top of the temple to represent John's prophecy (Hunter, J. Michael, "'I Saw Another Angel Fly,'" *Ensign*, Jan. 2000, p. 30).

Discussion Questions:

1. How is Moroni's message important to us? How is his message related to the gathering of Israel?

2. What do you think it would be like to be visited by an angel? Would you ever want to see an angel? Why or why not?

3. How can it help you to know that the gospel is "everlasting" (Rev. 14:6) and unchangeable? How might this influence your testimony of the gospel?

For Children:

Look up pictures of the varied statues of Moroni included on top of temple spires, including those by Cyrus Dallin, Torlief Knaphus, Millard F. Malin, and Avard Fairbanks. Ask the children what similarities and differences they see, or which one they like best. Share Revelation 14:6 with the children and explain that John's prophecy was fulfilled when Moroni appeared to the prophet Joseph Smith and restored the gospel. Ask, do you think John saw a vision of Moroni visiting Joseph Smith, or did he see temples with the statue of Moroni on the top? Explain.

150. Book of Life

The Apostle John mentions the book of life seven times in the Book of Revelation, but it's also mentioned in the Old Testament (Exodus 32:33), Book of Mormon (Alma 5:58), and Doctrine & Covenants (D&C 88:2). We learn in D&C 128:6-7 that the book of life is a heavenly record of the thoughts, words, and actions made of faithful saints during their lifetime. The book of life will be used during the Judgment Day to assess each person's life.

Discussion Questions:

1. What do you think a person has to do to get their name in the book of life? What sacrifices or callings would they have to make or fulfill?

2. Do you think it is possible for a person's name to be erased or deleted from the book of life? How does the repentance process influence what might be included in the book of life?

3. How is the book of life kept in heaven? Who do you imagine keeps the record up to date? How much detail is included?

For Children:

Read Revelation 20:12 together as a family. Explain that the book of life mentioned is a heavenly record of righteous men and women who have lived on the earth. Complete the following activity together: fold a piece of paper in half, and then into quarters to create a small "book." Have the children draw pictures or write down things about themselves that they think would be recorded in the book of life. Ask, what do you think a person has to do to be included in the book of life? Would you like to be recorded in the book of life? Why or why not?

Five Bonus Discussion Topics

151. Egypt

Egypt plays a significant and symbolic role in both the Old and New Testaments. Joseph was sold as a slave and taken into Egypt; later God raised up Moses to help free the Hebrew slaves being held captive there. In Matthew 2:13 and angel appears to Joseph, saying, "Arise, and take the young child and his mother, and flee into Egypt, and be thou there until I bring thee word: for Herod will seek the young child to destroy him." Joseph was obedient to this counsel and took his family to Egypt. After the danger had passed, they returned to Nazareth.

Discussion Questions:

1. Many stories in the Old Testament take place in Egypt. Which story is your favorite? Why?

2. What do you think Egypt symbolizes in the scriptures? How does the Lord use Egypt to influence the House of Israel?

3. Egypt played a key role in the Old Testament. What other influences has Egypt had in world history? Why do you think Egypt's influence has been so broad and deep?

For Children:

Use pictures from the Gospel Art Kit or the Church website to make a matching or memory game of Bible stories that take place in or involve Egypt. Let the children take turns reading or sharing the stories. Ask, which of these stories is your favorite? Why?

152. Tiberius Caesar

The Roman emperor on the throne during the last half of the Savior's life on earth was Tiberius Caesar. Tiberius Caesar, who had previously been a general, reigned from AD 14 to 37. He is mentioned by name in the Gospel of Luke. Tiberius Caesar's personality was dark and deeply corrupted, fulfilling prophecy by Isaiah that the Messiah would come to "The people that walked in darkness have seen a great light: they that dwell in the land of the shadow of death, upon them hath the light shined" (Isaiah 9:2).

Discussion Questions:

1. What impact does a wicked leader have on his or her people? How might Tiberius Caesar's wickedness have influenced Israel?

2. The Savior, asked if it was right to pay taxes to Tiberius Caesar, replied that taxes should be rendered to the government. What is a citizen's responsibility to government? How can we engage in a healthy political process?

3. How would you compare the darkness of Tiberius Caesar's time as emperor to world leaders today? What similarities and differences do you see?

For Children:

Have a bonfire after dark to roast marshmallows. Tell the children about Tiberius Caesar being a wicked emperor in Rome during Jesus' ministry. Share Isaiah 9:2 and explain that the people who walked in darkness were those under the rule of Tiberius Caesar and the light that shined was the Savior. Contrast the darkness of night to the light of the fire. Ask, what do you think it would be like to live under the rule of a wicked leader? How does Jesus Christ bring light into our lives?

153. Andrew

Andrew was one of the original twelve disciples chosen by Jesus Christ. In fact, tradition has it that Andrew was the very first disciple called by the Savior. Andrew is a brother to Simon Peter. Because his name is not Hebrew, but Greek, some historians believe there is a possibility of cultural diversity in Andrew's family. Andrew and Peter were both fishermen by trade and were called by the Savior to be "fishers of men" (Matt. 4:19). Prior to being a disciple, Andrew was a follower of John the Baptist.

Discussion Questions:

1. When John the Baptist told Andrew that Jesus was the Lamb of God, Andrew immediately believed. How can we better follow Andrew's childlike example of faith?

2. Andrew appears to have been actively seeking for truth in his life. What can we learn from Andrew's story to help those around us who are also seeking for truth?

3. Andrew is the disciple who first noticed a small boy had five small barley loaves and two small fish. How did being aware of his surroundings bless the lives of others? How can we be more aware of those we associate with?

For Children:

Play a game of follow the leader, changing of leaders to give each child a turn. After, complement each child for the different things they did as the leader. Tell the story of Andrew being a follower of John the Baptist, but then deciding to follow Jesus once he was told Christ was the Lamb of God. Ask, is it hard to start following a new leader, like Andrew did? Why was it important for Andrew to follow Jesus instead of John the Baptist?

154. Miracle of the Swine

During His travels to the Gadarenes, the Savior met a man who had been possessed by devils for a long time. When the possessed man saw Jesus, he fell at the feet of the Savior, saying, "Jesus, thou Son of God most high? I beseech thee, torment me not." When Jesus asked what his name was, the many devils in him identified as Legion and plead not to be cast out, asking instead to let them possess a herd of swine feeding nearby. The Savior cast the devils out of the man and allowed them to enter the swine; but the herd immediately charged down into a lake and drowned.

Discussion Questions:

1. The evil spirits clearly do not want to have to leave the body of the man they are possessing. Why do you think this is? What benefits does a body provide to a spirit?

2. The evil spirits immediately recognize Jesus as the Son of God. How do they recognize Him? Why did they call out to Jesus?

3. Why did the Savior let the evil spirits go into the swine? Why do you think the possessed swine immediately charged down the incline into the water?

For Children:

Use an online tutorial to teach your children how to draw a pig. While learning, explain that another name for pigs is swine. Recount the miracle of the swine to the children from Luke 8. Explain that the spirits were those who chose to follow Satan and did not to come to earth to get a body. Ask, why did the evil spirits want to stay in the man's body? What do you like about having a body?

155. Parable of the House Built Upon a Rock

"Therefore whosoever heareth these sayings of mine, and doeth them, I will liken him unto a wise man, which built his house upon a rock: And the rain descended, and the floods came, and the winds blew, and beat upon that house; and it fell not: for it was founded upon a crock. And every one that heareth these sayings of mine, and doeth them not, shall be likened unto a foolish man, which built his house upon the sand: And the rain descended, and the floods came, and the winds blew, and beat upon that house; and it fell: and great was the fall of it" (Matt. 7:24-27).

Discussion Questions:

1. In your opinion, how does a person build their testimony on the Savior, or on a rock? What is required to do so?

2. What do some people build their lives on that might be compared to sand? What do some people build their testimonies on that might be compared to sand?

3. Why would someone try to build a structure on sand? How can we overcome the common tendencies of laziness or taking shortcuts in life?

For Children:

Teach your children the song and motions for the Primary song "The Wise Man and the Foolish Man." After, explain that this song is based on a parable Jesus told people He was teaching in New Testament times. Read the parable, found in Matthew 7:24-27. Ask, why do rocks make a good place to build a house? What is it Jesus want us to build on the rock, or strong foundation?

Dear Reader,

Thank you for reading Let's Learn Together New Testament. I hope these study topics have been effective and have helped to enhance your Come, Follow Me study. In particular, I hope that you have noticed an increase in gospel- oriented conversations.

If you can spare a few minutes, I would be extremely grateful for a review from you on Goodreads or Amazon. Reviews make a huge difference in every aspect of publishing, so I'm incredibly grateful for those who take time to share their thoughts on these platforms.

Thanks again for your support.

Kind regards, Rebecca

Other books in this series:

Come Talk with Me: D&C

Let's Learn Together: Old Testament

Let's Learn Together: Book of Mormon
(Coming Fall 2023)

Other books by Rebecca Irvine:

Improving Family Communication

MTC at Home

Follow the Prophets

Family Home Evening Adventures

Adventures with the Word of God

About Rebecca Irvine

Rebecca Irvine is a graduate of Brigham Young University where she earned both bachelor's and master's degrees in Communications. She worked for over 15 years as a marketing research analyst for various ad agencies and PR firms. In addition to a love of writing, Irvine followed in her father's footsteps and became a college professor, currently teaching communication courses at Benedictine University and Scottsdale Community College. Rebecca is married and the mother of three amazing grown-up kids. Reading, walking, and bingeing Jane Austen films are some of her favorite activities.

Like me on Facebook: @Rebecca Irvine

Follow me on Instagram: @author.RebeccaIrvine

Acknowledgements

Several years ago, when the Come, Follow Me curriculum was just beginning, I had no plans to write a book to help families with their studies. But shortly after Christmas the idea for the first book, Come, Talk with Me: D&C, came to me. I began writing on a road trip to take my son up to BYU for the winter semester. Five weeks later I had a finished draft. Writing it was such a remarkable experience. I truly felt the light of the spirit while writing. I want to thank my Heavenly Father for the opportunity I have had to learn and write about these important concepts. It has truly been a blessing to be able to have the experience writing a similar version for each year of study. I am eternally grateful for being so blessed.

I also want to thank those who have provided me with feedback along the way. Without this love and support I would never have moved forward. Thank you to my ANWA critique group members for all the advice and support; you're the best! Thank you to Ruth for your editing assistance and Emily for cover design feedback. And an extra big thank you to my husband Steve for being the best sounding board/thesaurus ever!

Made in the USA
Las Vegas, NV
07 January 2023

65143390R00184